FLASHPOINT CHINA, Chinese air power and regional security

Andreas Rupprecht

FLASHPOINT CHINA

Chinese air power and regional security

Andreas Rupprecht

HARPIA
PUBLISHING+

2803 Sackett Street, Houston, TX 77098-1125, U.S.A.
flashpointchina@harpia-publishing.com

Consulting and inspiration by Kerstin Berger
Artworks and diagrams by Tom Cooper
Maps by James Lawrence
Editorial by Thomas Newdick
Layout by Norbert Novak, www.media-n.at, Vienna

Printed at Grasl FairPrint, Austria

Harpia Publishing, L.L.C. is a member of

ISBN 978-0-9854554-8-4

Contents

Acknowledgements

This book is the result of enthusiastic and intensive cooperation on the part of many individuals and several organisations. While in some cases the author does not feel free to mention individuals' names, and prefers to express his gratitude personally, it cannot be emphasised sufficiently that this work was made possible only thanks to many different people, who provided precious support, guidance and – most of all – patience in the process of developing this project.

The author's deepest gratitude is offered to a number of posters on various online discussion groups, without whose knowledge and assistance this work could never have been realised. The author would like to thank them all for their extensive help in the provision of references, sharing of literature, translations of original publications and documentation, research into the latest developments as well as their unstinting moral support.

Last but not least, the author would like to express his gratitude to his family, for their understanding and patience throughout the duration of what was a very intensive period of work.

Andreas Rupprecht, March 2016

Abbreviations

AAM	air-to-air missile
AB	Air Base
AD	Aviation/Air Division
ADIZ	Air Defence and Identification Zone
AEW&C	airborne early warning and control
AFAU	Air Force Aviation University
AR	Aviation Regiment
ASM	air-to-surface missile
ASW	anti-submarine warfare
BD	Bomber Division
BR	Bomber Regiment
BS	Bomber Squadron
BVR	beyond visual range
CAS	close air support
CCP	Chinese Communist Party
CFTE	China Flight Test Establishment
CMC	Central Military Commission
DCGS	Deputy Chief of the General Staff
det	detachment
DPC	Deputy Political Commissar
ECM	electronic countermeasures
ECS	East China Sea
EEZ	Exclusive Economic Zone
ELINT	electronic intelligence
ESM	electronic support measures
EW	electronic warfare
EO	electro-optical
FD	Fighter Division
GCI	ground-controlled interception
GPS	Global Positioning System
HALE	high altitude long endurance
HQ	headquarters
IFR	in-flight refuelling
INS	inertial navigation system
IR	infrared
LGB	laser-guided bomb
MND	Ministry of National Defence
MR	Military Region
MRAF	Military Region Air Force
n/a	no information available
NAD	Naval Aviation Division
nm	nautical miles
ORBAT	order of battle
PLA	People's Liberation Army
PLAAF	People's Liberation Army Air Force

PLAN	People's Liberation Army Navy
PLANAF	People's Liberation Army Naval Air Force
PRC	People's Republic of China
RoC	Republic of China (Taiwan)
SAM	surface-to-air missile
SAR	search and rescue
SCS	South China Sea
SEAD	suppression of enemy air defences
SIGINT	signals intelligence
TFG	Tactical Fighter Group
TFW	Tactical Fighter Wing
UAV	unmanned aerial vehicle
UCAV	unmanned combat aerial vehicle
UK	United Kingdom
unc.	unconfirmed
US	United States
USAF	United States Air Force
USD	US Dollar
USN	United States Navy (includes US Naval Aviation)
USSR	Union of Soviet Socialist Republics
VKS	Russian Aerospace Forces (Vozdushno-Kosmicheskie Sily)

INTRODUCTION

The background to this volume is relatively straightforward. Drawing upon the comprehensive presentation of the equipment and organisation of the People's Liberation Army Air Force (PLAAF) and the People's Liberation Army Naval Air Force (PLANAF) provided in the book *Modern Chinese Warplanes* (Harpia Publishing, 2012), this study offers an overview of potential military conflicts along the borders of the People's Republic of China (PRC).

Decades of relative isolation, the language barrier, and the clearly observable progress made by the PRC's military – the People's Liberation Army (PLA) – in the last two decades have resulted in increasing interest in this subject around the world, and thousands of related publications. However, while most of these merely list new equipment acquisitions, very few discuss in any depth the operational histories of the Chinese military, and even fewer embark on detailed discussions of PLAAF and PLANAF capabilities and intentions. Consequently, there is still very little understanding about when, where and why the PRC has in the past decided to wage military conflicts. The purpose of this volume is to offer a short historic introduction to each of the regional 'powder kegs' in question, and to summarise PLAAF and PLANAF – and in some cases PLA Army Aviation – orders of battle (ORBATs) in the relevant geographical areas.

It is noteworthy that the topics in question have been the subject of vigorous debate for some 20 years. Most of these are fuelled by the interconnecting interests of the PRC, the Republic of China (RoC, in this study Taiwan), India, Japan, and numerous local powers, but also by the dramatic economic growth in the region and a number of mutual disputes, as well as the diminished influence of the United States and Russian Federation (as successor to the former Soviet Union).

Where exactly this might lead is uncertain. What is clear is that by the early 1990s the PRC was already expressing its displeasure at the existence of an 'Asian solar system' in which the US alone played the role of the sun. Around the same time, the higher echelons of the PLA publicly acknowledged that they perceived a historical opportunity to build up a modern military force. Ever since, the PRC has run an accelerated and large-scale military modernisation programme, made possible by dramatic economic and technological advances.

Over the last few years, the combined effects of these developments have provided the first clear indications of power projection initiated by Beijing in centuries. In turn, such behaviour threatens to disturb the 'status quo' imposed in the wider Asia-Pacific region since the end of World War II, and has the very serious potential to provoke a major international crisis.

China's self-perception

From the mountains on the frontier with Nepal, to the near-endless plains along the border with Mongolia, and from the forests bordering Russia's Far East to the South China Sea, the continued economic rise of the PRC has led to a dramatic shift in the balance of power in the region. As a result, the relationship between the PRC and its neighbours, as well as with the US and it allies, is becoming increasingly important for the future of the region and for the rest of the world. Few had expected China's economy to grow as quickly, and its advances in the military realm have also come as a surprise to many.

Consequently, many observers – especially those in the West – consider China's behaviour to be 'aggressive', while many of its neighbours have expressed their outright fear of so-called 'Chinese expansionism', and 'communism'. Indeed, one of the biggest problems is that in the Western mainstream media, and even in most Western think tanks – which are nowadays ever more influential in policy-making – China is seen from a purely Western standpoint. A lack of general understanding, combined with entirely different perceptions, cultural differences, and language barriers, but also a lack of official transparency in regard to the PLA's capabilities and intentions, all combine to result in no little fear of the PRC's rapidly growing military.

All of this makes the strategic situation in the region as dynamic as it is complicated. In fact – and while there is little doubt that China is challenging the US and its allies, especially so in the South China Sea, but also in the East China Sea and in cyberspace – such feelings are generally mutual. In fact, many Chinese know as little about the West – and especially about the US – as Westerners generally know about the PRC. Not surprisingly, they view the West – and the US in particular – with suspicion, even more so because certain US allies in Asia have acted aggressively towards China in the past.

Understanding modern-day points of view in China requires not only an understanding of the history of the country, but also its self-perception. From its own standpoint, China has been a pawn in a game played by external powers for nearly two centuries, before Japan invaded and committed wartime atrocities. In particular during the late 19th and the first half of the 20th century – often described as the 'century of humiliation' in the PRC – each of these powers carved out its own spheres of influence, in turn weakening Chinese sovereignty either by war, or by enforced concessions. After decades of external humiliation and often bloody internal unrest, and decades of social and economic austerity, the country is finally recovering its prestige and power, much of which have been forgotten elsewhere. In turn, this has enabled the PRC to begin recovering significant parts of its territories, so many of which were lost in what China describes as 'unequal treaties'. This not only included large swathes of continental borders, but above all the PRC's maritime frontier. Consequently, the idea that China is only now expanding its maritime claims as a result of its new-found power is not borne out by the facts. On the contrary, after centuries of weakness, the country is finally in a position and willing to act 'robustly' – in exactly the same fashion as many other states would – as it seeks to recover what it sees as pre-existing sovereignty claims that have been in place for decades.

Therefore, it is clear that China sees its rise today not as that of an imperialist or expansionist power, but that of a power that is regaining and securing what is its own. For similar reasons, China feels that the US and some of its allies especially

are holding it back from regaining the traditional, central role it previously played in regional and global affairs. According to the Chinese viewpoint, these external powers have attempted to restrict the PRC's development in order to maintain their own hegemony.

The modern-day Chinese perception of sovereignty is based on similar experiences. Many influential Chinese represent the standpoint that their country's sovereignty was restored only by the Communist Party in 1949, and that the PRC subsequently found itself facing a world order shaped by the domination of the US and its allies. Because of this, China frequently views modern 'international laws and regulations' with suspicion: from the standpoint of the PRC, these are a Western invention, based on Western moral understandings. More than a few Chinese do not feel bound by any kind of international conventions – especially not those created without their participation, or at least without their input or consent. On the contrary, for them it is important to insist that all countries accept the PRC's claims to territorial sovereignty over the territories it controls, including those parts of the country where non-ethnic Chinese are dominant, and especially over Taiwan.

Therefore the reality is not so much that China is seeking to expand its territory, as much as it is unwilling to recognise or respect international norms or the sovereignty of others, especially so in cases where local interests interfere with the PRC's interests. Correspondingly, the PRC is not only modernising and strengthening its military in order to protect its sovereignty and related claims, but is simultaneously pursuing legal and diplomatic avenues to circumvent US spheres of influence and to establish its own.

Clearly, this interpretation should not be misunderstood as a call to 'understand the Chinese world view', nor an offer for solutions to the many different points of contention between the PRC and its various neighbours. However, a knowledge and understanding of such points of view might help provide a more balanced overview of China's aims and ambitions. Regardless what the US or any of its allies deem to be Chinese intentions – and regardless of whether these are considered 'legitimate' or 'historically comprehensible' by the international community or not – China is unlikely to cede most of its claims, especially so in the case of Taiwan and the South China Sea. The earlier such standpoints are accepted, the better, because this might provide the best opportunity to accommodate the PRC's 'return' as a great power, in turn de-escalating the situation, and enabling a closer integration of the country into international and multilateral frameworks.

The PLAAF remains the third largest air force in the world, after the United States Air Force (USAF), and the Russian Aerospace Forces (Vozdushno-Kosmicheskie Sily, VKS). Indeed, despite some down sizing and reorganisation, it is likely to become the world's second largest air force by the end of this decade. Like the rest of the PLA, it continues to pursue a long-term, comprehensive modernisation programme designed to improve its capability to fight and win a short-duration, high-intensity regional military conflict, or a 'limited war under high-tech conditions'. The principal focus in this process remains on protecting China's sovereignty and territorial integrity, and preparing for a potential conflict in the Taiwan Strait. However, there is little doubt that the interests of the Chinese air arm – like those of the entire PLA – have meanwhile expanded well beyond this goal, and now include efforts to obtain greater influence in the international system.

Chinese self-perception also dictates the way this book is organised. Namely, from the standpoint of the average Western observer, China's neighbours are usually grouped according to Northern Asia (including Mongolia and Russia), the Far East (Japan, the Koreas and Taiwan), Southeast Asia (Indonesia, Laos, the Philippines and Vietnam), South Asia (Afghanistan, Bhutan, India, Myanmar, Nepal and Pakistan) and Central Asia (Kazakhstan, Kyrgyzstan and Tajikistan). The PLA assigns responsibilities for these areas in an entirely different fashion. For example, the borders with Mongolia and Russia are assigned to the same Northern Theater Command – together with the Central Theater Command – that is also responsible for the area facing the Korean peninsula and Japan. Otherwise, the responsibility for the borders in the complete southern and western sector including all Southwest Asian countries, and all those within the Himalayas and the former Soviet Republics are united within the Western Theater Command.

As a result, the usual alphabetic order is replaced by a geographical system starting with Mongolia and Russia and following clockwise from the north. By treating the countries in this order, it is possible to follow the PLA structure, which enables a clearer understanding of the corresponding ORBATs, and also to avoid confusion and repetition. The following ORBATs only list the most important operational units in terms of combat and combat support, including transport and special mission units. Training units including the Flying Academies and the Aviation University as well as the different Flight Test and Training units are not listed. However, in regions where no major PLAAF or PLANAF units are based – above all in the Western Theater Command – Army Aviation units are also mentioned and their equipment listed when this comprises the most important types assigned.

The following table shows the countries and territories in clockwise order beginning in the north:

Theater Command	Related countries/territory
Northern Theater Command (北部战区) Central Theater Command (中部战区)	Mongolia Russia North Korea and South Korea Japan
Eastern Theater Command (东部战区)	Taiwan East China Sea
Southern Theater Command (南部战区)	South China Sea Vietnam Laos Myanmar
Western Theater Command (西部战区)	Bhutan Nepal India Pakistan Afghanistan Tajikistan Kyrgyzstan Kazakhstan

Key

- ● PLAAF Command Posts
- ● PLANAF HQs
- MR Former Military Region

▶ A map of China showing the five new PLAAF and three PLANAF theater commands as well as the previous seven military regions (dotted grey line).
(Map by Lames Lawerence)

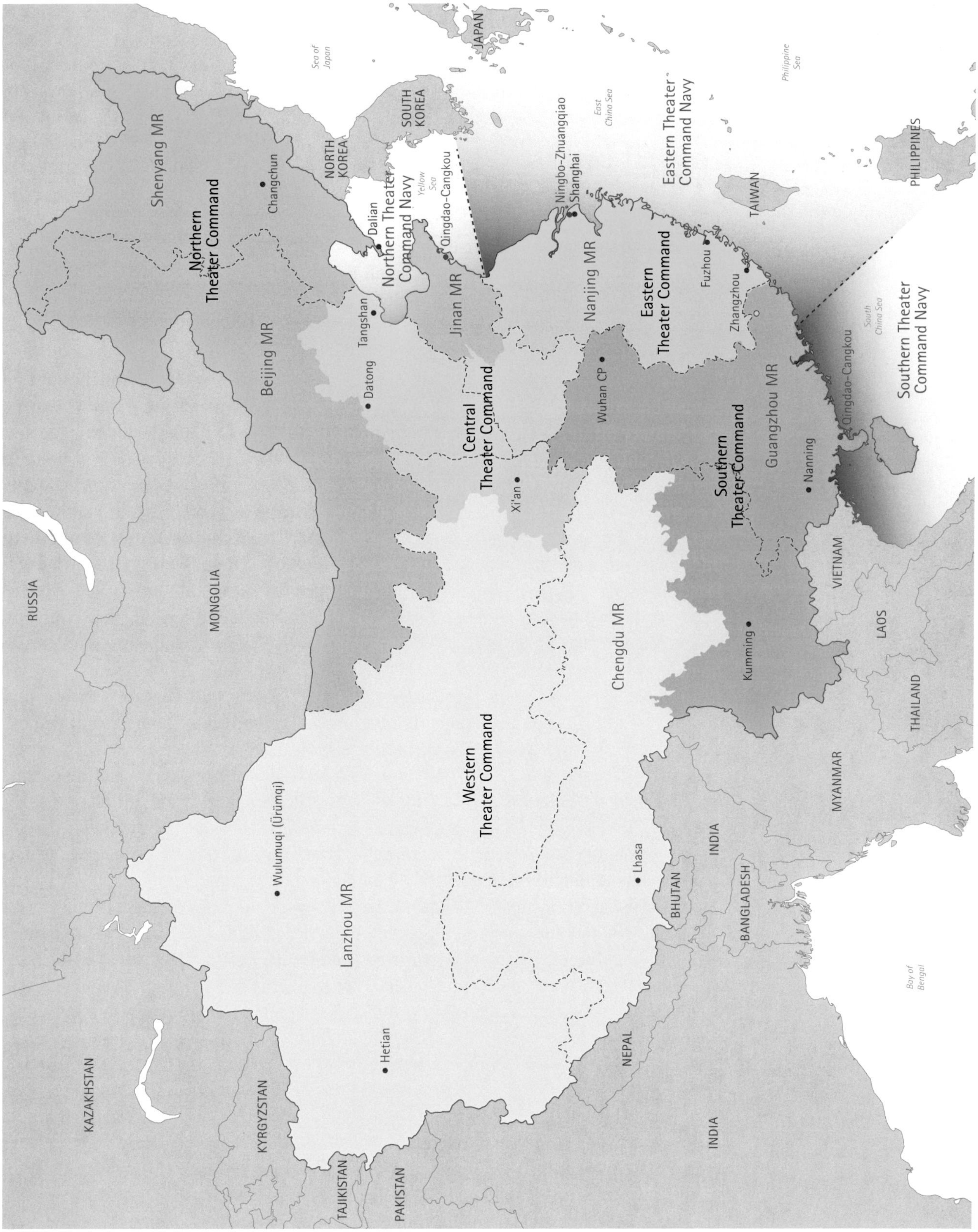
Northern Theater Command
Shenyang MR
Changchun
Beijing MR
Datong
Tangshan
Dalian
Northern Theater Command Navy
Yellow Sea
Qingdao-Cangkou
Jinan MR
Central Theater Command
Xi'an
Nanjing MR
Ningbo-Zhuangqiao
Shanghai
East China Sea
Eastern Theater Command
Eastern Theater Command Navy
Fuzhou
Zhangzhou
Wuhan CP
Southern Theater Command
Guangzhou MR
Nanning
Qingdao-Cangkou
South China Sea
Southern Theater Command Navy
Kumming
Chengdu MR
Lhasa
Western Theater Command
Lanzhou MR
Wulumuqi (Ürümqi)
Hetian
RUSSIA
MONGOLIA
KAZAKHSTAN
KYRGYZSTAN
TAJIKISTAN
PAKISTAN
INDIA
NEPAL
BHUTAN
BANGLADESH
INDIA
MYANMAR
THAILAND
LAOS
VIETNAM
PHILIPPINES
TAIWAN
NORTH KOREA
SOUTH KOREA
JAPAN
Sea of Japan
Philippine Sea
Bay of Bengal

Left: Perhaps no other type better represents the PLAAF's expanding ambitions than the J-20. After its first flight in early 2011, the serial production phase was attained within five years, as demonstrated by the first initial-production aircraft, serial number '2101'. (Top81.cn)

Right: The Y-9JB – also known as the Y-8GX-8 – is a dedicated intelligence-gathering aircraft featuring an advanced integrated ELINT system similar to that in the US Navy's EP-3. This type flies routine ELINT missions over the East China Sea facing Japan. (FYJS)

Modernisation, strategy, structural changes

Somewhat surprisingly, China's recent White Paper references for the first time 'China's Military Strategy'. Here, the leadership of the PLA clearly acknowledges its growing self-confidence and pride as an emerging global power that enjoys its international standing. The defined Core National Objectives are, in short, to secure national unity (security and stability), China's territorial integrity (a clear hint to Taiwan) and to protect national interests, including securing China's overseas interests, its strategic sea lines of communication (SLOCs); the result is a de facto description of the 'Dual Silk Road initiative'. As a consequence, for China, security along these lines is as vital as American insistence on freedom of navigation through the South China Sea, which for China presents an opportunity to circumvent the growing containment and encirclement embodied by the US 'pivot to Asia'.

In order to accomplish its military tasks, the PLA is undertaking a major programme of reform; this addresses training and education, development and acquisition of modern weapons systems and equipment, the way these systems are operated, and structural reform of the overall command system. For the first time in its history, the PLAAF will attempt to shift its focus from primarily territorial air defence to the ability to conduct offensive and defensive operations as well. This includes – and in the public, this element naturally receives the most attention – the introduction of new hardware including modern multirole-capable combat types (J-10B/C, J-15, J-16) and special mission aircraft (Y-8GX family) and the development of next-generation types (J-20, FC-31, unmanned aircraft). Equally importantly, it also includes the build-up of expeditionary forces to project power over long distances. However, perhaps the most important reforms are largely unnoticed and are related to tactics and training. These have also been undergoing a rapid transformation and will probably be much more important in a future conflict than the sheer quantity of new hardware. In parallel to the PLAAF, the People's Liberation Army Navy (PLAN) and especially the PLANAF will probably transform even more dramatically, emphasising a greater focus on the high seas, including an expanded naval role beyond the previously established sphere. In this regard, China has to establish itself as a major regional maritime power. To achieve that, the PLAN will shift its focus from offshore waters defence (brown-water force) to an open seas protection (blue-water force). For some years the PLAN has invested heavily in submarines and surface combatants, and above all in an indigenous (second) aircraft carrier, but also in modern fighters, bombers and special mission aircraft.

Left: An anonymous serial-production J-16 photographed during a pre-delivery flight. The first operational unit for this multirole type is the 175th Brigade within the Flight Test and Training Centre (FTTC). Unconfirmed reports suggested a regiment within the 3rd Fighter Division was under transition as of March 2016. (Weibo)

Right: While the regular JL-9 entered service in 2007, this rarely seen PLANAF JL-9A is a dedicated naval trainer, developed to train pilots to operate on board an aircraft carrier. The JL-9A entered service with the Naval Aviation Air Academy in late 2013. (Top81.cn)

Another key component of China's active defence strategy is the so-called element of anti-access/area denial (A2/AD) capabilities. This strategy in particular concerns China's current inferiority in terms of its military capabilities and weapons systems in comparison to a technologically superior opponent. This strategy is of greatest importance in the current South China Sea situation, since its goal is to deny freedom of movement/action across the range of military operations; here especially it would serve to deny the US military the ability to operate in China's littoral waters in case of a crisis. Therefore, especially in the US, strategies and operational concepts to counter China's A2/AD capabilities tend to focus on ways the US can gain access to and operate within China's littoral waters.

Perhaps most importantly, the PLA's current pattern of deployment is entirely inconsistent with a force structure intended to conduct offensive operations far from national borders. In order to better implement its strategic goals, the PLA's seven historical Military Regions (Beijing, Chengdu, Guangzhou, Jinan, Lanzhou, Nanjing and Shenyang) and their commands had ceased to exist by early 2016 and had been replaced by five new Theater Commands – formerly also known as Strategic Zones – Northern, Central, Eastern, Southern and Western). Based on the latest information, the previous entities were planned to be dismantled by the end of 2015 and general reforms were implemented by 1 February 2016. Although not all aspects have been revealed – especially in terms of geographical distribution or assignment of certain PLAAF units – this restructuring is part of a long-planned, far-reaching overhaul, the aim of which is to shift the PLA from the former army-centric system towards a Western-style joint command, in which the Army, Navy and Air Force are equally represented.

The 'Divine Eagle' – or Project 973 – is a large HALE-type UAV under development at the No. 601 Institute in Shenyang since around 2010–12. Its main role will be to provide real-time intelligence over vast ocean and coastal regions as well as continuous maritime surveillance over the South China Sea and the East China Sea ADIZ. (Top81.cn)

Left: The Hongdu L-15 - designated JL-10 in Chinese service - is one of the most important new types in terms of modernising PLAAF flight training. Seen here is the fifth prototype, under test at the CFTE. (Top81.cn)

Right: Like the J-20, the XAC Y-20 is a project of national prestige. It aims to develop a strategic transport capable of deploying forces and materiel over vast distances. This particular aircraft is the third prototype. (Top81.cn)

Conclusions and consequences

In conclusion, it can be summarised that within the past two decades, China's military – both in terms of strategic considerations and the modernisation of procedures and materiel – has undergone some of the most profound reforms since its establishment. Globally, this demonstrates that China no longer wants to be a second-rate player; it wants to take a lead role in politics within its sphere of influence using alliances it has formed itself as well as multilateral institutions. Above all, China wants to establish a new system that offers an alternative to the current global network based on Western architecture. It is for this reason that the rival interests of China and the US collide in the Pacific region.

In the West, most observers have focused on growing Chinese military capabilities and new weapons systems. However, even if China can be deemed assertive and provocative, a call to understand China's world view is certainly not an argument for appeasement. While such an understanding does not present solutions – especially not easy ones – to the current issues, it could provide at least a more nuanced guide to Chinese goals and the external response to its actions. One thing is certain, and it is a fact that all players in the region will have to recognise: in the long term, stability in the region is solely achievable by integrating China within the greater international networks, and not through a policy of containment. After all, the main interests of all parties involved are very much the same – stability, security and freedom – as we all live in a globalised world.

Two Batch 01 production J-10Bs at Chengdu. While the aircraft in the background was awaiting delivery to the 2nd Division, the aircraft in front features the new WS-10B engine. By early 2016, 55 J-10B and 35 J-10C aircraft had been manufactured in two batches, most of which powered by the original AL-31FN Series 3 engines. (Top81.cn)

NORTHERN THEATER COMMAND & CENTRAL THEATER COMMAND

In the last 30 years, China's relationships with Russia and Mongolia – and also with Afghanistan and the various former republics of the Soviet Union, including Kazakhstan, Kyrgyzstan, and Tajikistan – were characterised by finding solutions to the various border disputes, some of which dates back to the 19th century. This approach included maintaining good diplomatic and economic ties, and otherwise not interfering in internal politics. Beijing is interested in maintaining stability and security in Northern and Central Asia not only for economic reasons, but also to avoid potential instability as a result of separatists.

The PLA subordinates responsibility for Japan and the Korean peninsula to the Northern Theater Command and to the Central Theater Command. Due to the very different political issues at stake, these Far Eastern countries are treated separately in this analysis. Stability and the avoidance of military conflict on the Korean peninsula appear to be among the top priorities for the government in Beijing. Nevertheless, the PRC apparently remains unable to find mutually satisfactory solutions for the disputes related to the East China Sea (ECS) that involve Japan and South Korea.

Mongolia

Mongolia has only two neighbours: Russia in the north and the PRC in the south. It shares 4,677km (2,906 miles) of its borders with China. Although its territory has shifted a number of times over the centuries, and despite its siding with the former USSR during the years of Sino-Soviet disputes, Mongolia has experienced no border disputes with either Beijing or Moscow since the 1960s. On the contrary, current relations between the PRC and Mongolia can be described as good, with mutual respect for sovereignty and independence. The two countries cooperate closely in counter-terrorist operations, and a mutual conflict is very unlikely.

This Mi-24V, based at Nalayh, is one of the few remaining air assets of the Mongolian People's Air Force. (Russian Ministry of Defence)

Russia

The second longest part of China's border – 4,209km (2,615 miles) in all – is shared with Russia. This border is divided into two sections: a long northeastern part of 4,195km (2,607 miles) and a much shorter western section that is around 40–55km (25–34 miles) long. For years, relations between China and Russia have been described as a 'tightrope walk', and have frequently oscillated between close friendship and war. For

A Russian Air Force Su-35S fighter from the 6987th Air Base in Komsomolsk-on-Amur in Russia's Far East. (Piotr Butowski)

most of the 1950s, Beijing and Moscow were close friends, but after the split of 1961, the two countries experienced nearly two decades of disputes, and a small-scale war in late 1960. It was only after lengthy negotiations that the PRC and the USSR finally defined their mutual border in 1991. This included 26 border crossings (including four for railways). However, the Soviet Union was dissolved only a few months later and China was thus forced to renegotiate its borders with Kyrgyzstan, Russia and Tajikistan. While negotiations with the former Soviet republics were concluded relatively quickly, those between Beijing and Moscow lasted for many more years. An agreement concerning the shorter part of the border – the stretch between the Altai Republic of the Russia and the Xinjiang Uyghur Autonomous Region of the PRC – was signed in May 1994, and the demarcation completed in 1998. A final series of supplemental agreements concerning the rest of the border were only signed in 2004, ratified in 2005, and demarcation was concluded in October 2008. Interestingly, the government of Taiwan refused to accept these treaties and continues its claim to some of the territories Beijing ceded to Moscow.

Economic and political cooperation was finally consolidated through the Shanghai Cooperation Organisation (SCO), signed in 1996, and including the PRC and Russia, as well as Kazakhstan, Kyrgyzstan, Tajikistan and (since 2001) Uzbekistan. The SCO ensures mutual respect for the national sovereignty of the countries involved (a particularly sensitive issue for the governments in Beijing and Moscow especially), but also provides a framework for close cooperation in regard to multilateral diplomacy, and cooperation in culture, economy, education, energy, science, technology and transportation. More recently, closer military links have been established between the militaries of the SCO countries, as exemplified by several joint exercises – primarily related to counter-terrorism operations, but also to air warfare.

From the PRC's standpoint, another area favourably regulated by the SCO is cooperation in high-technology industry, especially in regard to spaceflight and military aviation. After 1989 the cancellation of many highly promising cooperative projects with Western powers left China without a reliable provider of high technology. This was one of the major reasons why the PRC subsequently became a major customer of Russian military hardware. Despite the SCO, there some disagreements about this plan still exist between Beijing and Moscow, especially because Chinese companies tend to ignore or circumvent Russian copyrights, and have repeatedly developed and produced copies of Russian designs. Nevertheless, Russian interest in promoting business with China, and Chinese interest in obtaining Russian high technology both remain strong, and all related concerns have repeatedly been negotiated away. As a result the PRC continues to place major new orders with Russia – as illustrated by orders in 2015 for S-400 surface-to-air missiles (SAMs) and Su-35 multirole fighters.

Capabilities and intentions: Central and Northern Asia

Based on the generally cordial relations between the PRC and all of its neighbours in the last 20 years, and especially in light of direct military cooperation with Russia, mutual conflicts in the region are very unlikely. The Chinese side of the borders with its neighbours in Central and Northern Asia (Russia and Mongolia) was controlled by (from west to east) the former Lanzhou and Beijing Military Regions, of which the

Superseded by the modern H-6K in the strategic role, the H-6H still forms the backbone of the PLAAF bomber fleet. Seen here armed with a pair of KD-63 land attack cruise missiles, this H-6H is in service with the 36th Bomber Division, Central Theater Command. (Top81.cn)

latter is the most powerful and most important. Following the new organisation, the former Lanzhou MR became the Western Theater Command (see Chapter 5), while the former Beijing and Shenyang MRs were reorganised as the Northern and Central Theater Commands that now also cover Japan and the Koreas (discussed later in this chapter). That said, neither the PLA nor the PLAAF maintains any major units close to the borders of any Chinese neighbours in Central and Northern Asia, while the majority of PLAAF units assigned to the Lanzhou and Beijing Military Region Air Forces (MRAF) operate only point-defence interceptors and training aircraft. The sole exception to this rule is the 36th Bomber Division, which may be considered the PRC's 'silver bullet' force. Two of this division's regiments are equipped with H-6H bombers armed with land attack cruise missiles, but – according to officials in Beijing – they are not provided with nuclear warheads.

Since 2005, China and Russia have run joint military exercises under the name Peace Mission. Including up to 8,000 Chinese and 2,000 Russian troops, and air, land and sea elements, these usually simulate an intervention in a country in a state of political turmoil, and include establishment of aerial and naval blockades, amphibious assaults, and deployment of ground troops for the purpose of occupying a region. While some Western observers argue that this series of exercises is designed to intimidate Taiwan, others consider that it is used to test a possible scenario in case of the collapse of the government in North Korea.

Although Russia is seeking to use its influence within the SCO to undermine competing Western security projects, and while different joint exercises have been regularly run by SCO members since 2005, this organisation should not be understood as part of an evolving military pact. While sometimes involving Tu-22M and Tu-95MS strategic bombers and airborne early warning and control (AEW&C) aircraft from the VKS, most of these exercises are related to combating terrorism, and in this regard they are Beijing's and Moscow's 'message to the West'. They demonstrate that member states are in a position to effectively deal with any kind of emerging threats in Central Asia, without foreign assistance or influence.

Finally, the Chinese language – and the related shortage of suitable translators and teachers in member states – represents a significant challenge to more intensive military cooperation, while terrorism – usually resulting from separatism and oppression-induced extremism – is most likely to remain the principal threat to SCO members for the foreseeable future.

North Korea

Armed with R-27 AAMs, two DPRK MiG-29s from Unit 1017, 57th Air Regiment line up for take-off at Sunchan air base. (KCNA)

North Korea shares 1,416km (880 miles) of its border with China, a boundary that is primarily defined by two rivers, the Yalu and Tumen. The PRC has traditionally maintained friendly relations with North Korea (or, to give it its full name, the Democratic People's Republic of Korea – DPRK). These were forged early during the Korean War and only a year after the establishment of the PRC. The primary reasoning for this position appears not to be ideological rivalry with Japan, South Korea or the US, but a fear of the negative effects of a North Korean collapse. This in turn is connected to concerns about potentially millions of North Koreans attempting to flee to the PRC, or starving to death due to famine.

Knowing full well that North Korean provocations and seemingly short-sighted military actions are in fact attempts to gain a degree of political attention on the international scene, the government in Beijing remains patient with its partners in Pyongyang. At the same time, it urges South Korea and the US not to push North Korea too hard. Another reason for this stance is the fact that North Korea could easily provoke a war with South Korea and the US, and that the PRC would be inevitably drawn into any major military confrontation, a result of obligations stemming from a military treaty signed between Beijing and Pyongyang in 1961.

South Korea

The PRC and South Korea do not share any mutual borders, but the position of the latter is relevant not only because of the close partnership between China and North Korea, and differing ideological and political systems, but above all because of South Korea's alliance with the US, and its strategic position in proximity to Japan.

The PRC and South Korea only established diplomatic relations in 1992. Previously, their relations were severely hampered by experiences from the Korean War, and the decades of mutual non-recognition that followed. More recently, the two nations have expanded their economic relations, which has in turn led to a deterioration of relations between South Korea and Taiwan. Nevertheless, the governments in Beijing and Seoul still differ in regard to issues related to the control of airspace and sea areas in the East China Sea (ECS), and in regard to their respective exclusive economic zones (EEZs) located there. More precisely, there is a dispute between the PRC and South Korea concerning the status of the so-called Socotra Rock, a submerged reef about 149km (80 miles) southwest of Marado in South Korea, known as Suyan Rock in China and Ieodo (also as Parangdo) in South Korea.

Two South Korean F-15K Slam Eagles from the 11th Tactical Fighter Wing at Daegu Air Base. (USAF/SSgt Jason Colbert)

According to the UN's Convention on the Law of the Sea (UNCLOS) from 2009, no country has the right to claim this reef as its own territory. However, Beijing and Seoul are in dispute over which side is in a position to claim it as within its own EEZ. For example, Beijing strongly protested South Korea's construction of the Ieodo Ocean Research Station on Socotra Rock, which included a helipad.

The issue of the Socotra Rock is related to another dispute between the two countries: that of the Air Defence and Identification Zone (ADIZ) maintained over this area by South Korea. Originally established by the USAF during the Korean War, the ADIZ in question covers most of the airspace claimed by South Korea, with the exception of few remote areas. After China declared its own ADIZ over the southern portion of the ECS in 2013, South Korea declared an expansion of its zone to include the islands of Marado and Hongdo, in addition to Socotra Rock, in December of the same year.

Japan

Two giants of the Far East, the PRC and Japan share a long historical relationship and are now the two largest economies in Asia. Historically, China always exercised a strong influence upon Japanese culture, law, philosophy and religion, and the two countries share a deeply rooted understanding of honour, national pride, respect and recurring references to history. A rift appeared only under the influence of Western imperial powers in the 19th century, to which Japan reacted with a dramatic modernisation of its economy and society, while the central government of China collapsed. The country became not only a scene to a decades-long civil war, but found itself exposed to humiliating Japanese invasions. The latter remain the primary reason for Beijing's poor relations with Tokyo, especially because Japan continues to refuse to offer an official apology for atrocities committed in China between 1894 and 1945. The situation has deteriorated continuously since 2010, when Japan began accusing China of withholding important reserves of valuable rare earth elements, while the PLA began confronting Japan in the ECS. The dispute over the Senkaku Islands – known as the Diaoyu Islands in China – is meanwhile a matter of heated rhetoric and near-open hostility.

Connected to the nature of relations between the PRC and Japan is also the issue of Taiwan. In 1895, what was then known as the island of Formosa was permanently ceded by China to Japan, together with the Pescadores island group (known as Penghu in China). After Japan's defeat in 1945, Japanese troops surrendered to the representa-

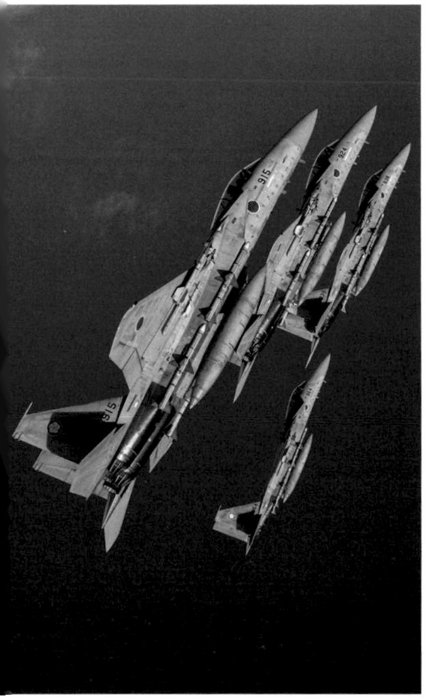

Some 150 F-15Js form the backbone of Japan's aerial defences. These four fully armed F-15Js are from the 305th Hikotai, based at Hyakuri. (Katsuhiko Tokunaga/DACT, Inc.)

tives of the Supreme Allied Commander in the China Theater, Chinese General Chiang Kai-shek. In turn, when Chiang Kai-shek's Nationalist forces were defeated by the Communists at the end of the Chinese Civil War, in the 1949–50 period, they withdrew to Taiwan to establish their own state, officially the Republic of China (RoC). This was considered the sole legitimate government of China even by the UN until 1971.

Meanwhile, Japan regained its sovereignty with the conclusion of the San Francisco Peace Treaty (SFPT) in 1952, and renounced all claims to Formosa/Taiwan, the Pescadores, as well as the Spratly and Paracel Islands. However, the US failed to invite the governments of either Taiwan or the PRC to the SFPT: the Communists were not considered the legitimate government of China, while the Nationalists were not in control of Mainland China. Under intense US pressure, Japan and Taiwan subsequently concluded the Treaty of Taipei, formally ending the Second Sino-Japanese War (fought 1937–45). Beijing never accepted this act, and insists that the government of the PRC be recognised as the sole legitimate government of China. Furthermore, the US retained the Senkaku Islands as firing ranges and later gave responsibility back to Japan, and not to China.

To make matters even more complex, in 1972 Beijing and Tokyo re-established official diplomatic relations. Ever since, Japan has acknowledged the PRC government as the 'sole government of China', in exchange for the PRC renouncing war reparations owed by Japan. Both governments declared the Treaty of Taipei as invalid, and Tokyo broke off diplomatic relations with Taiwan. However, it does retain non-governmental, working-level relations.

The third factor complicating Sino-Japanese relations is the deep political and military partnership between Japan and the US. Ever since ratifying the Treaty of Mutual Cooperation and Security (TMCS) of 1960, Japan has been the most important US strategic partner in the region. This treaty not only provided security guarantees for Japan in exchange for a continuous US military presence, but it also included general provisions that became the basis for the subsequent expansion of the Japanese economy. More recently, the continued importance of this partnership was signalled by several US officials, who repeatedly stressed their position that the Senkaku Islands fall under Japanese administrative jurisdiction and thus within the scope of the TMCS.

The latest decisions by the government in Tokyo have reconsidered previous standpoints including the country's pacifist constitution. This potentially opens the way for the Japanese to play a more assertive role in the increasingly tense region, and could permit the Japanese military to become involved in foreign conflicts for the first time since 1945. Combined with the growth of Chinese military power, all these factors contribute significantly to the fact that, despite a number of common interests, the PRC and the US consider each other as potential adversaries, as much as strategic partners.

Capabilities and intentions: North and Northeast Asia

Responsible for the northern sector of this vast area is the Northern Theater Command, which includes the former Shenyang MRAF and parts of the Beijing MR. The Central Theater Command is responsible for the northeastern part, formerly consisting of the remaining parts of the Beijing MR, parts of the Jinan MR and parts of the

Left: The PLAAF has converted several Tu-154Ms into dedicated ELINT aircraft as the Tu-154M/D, and these are used to monitor neighbouring countries. Their main mission is to conduct ELINT around the East China Sea, near Japan. Four aircraft are operational and at least three more were under conversion in early 2016. (Japan Ministry of Defense)

Right: The Y-8J (Project 515) is a first-generation AEW&C platform featuring the British Searchwater 2000 surveillance radar in its characteristic bulbous nose radome. Four examples are operational in PLANAF service and are regularly seen flying ELINT missions over the East China Sea, facing Japan. (Japan Ministry of Defense)

Guangzhou MR. To be precise, the small westernmost part of the Sino-Russian border falls within the responsibility of the new Western Theater Command – the former Lanzhou MR – but is of minimal importance.

Overall, both new theater commands are responsible for air defence of the entire border between the PRC and Russia, from North Korea southwards up to the Shandong/Jaingsu provincial border. Especially important is the capital Beijing, and the major city of Tianjin. Additional tasks include the training of key personnel for top leadership positions and some maintenance of certain crucial PLAAF test facilities. Consequently, the units in this area are equipped with a well-balanced mix of interceptors, fighter-bombers, and support aircraft, including a wide range of electronic and signals intelligence (ELINT/SIGINT) gatherers in the form of different variants of the Y-8 transport. Additionally, the theater commands are responsible for coverage of the Chinese coast around the Yellow Sea. The PLA's important 15th Airborne Army is based in the same area, but is directly subordinated to the HQ in Beijing.

PLANAF units in this area are deployed on bases along the northern part of the ECS (Yellow Sea) and thus cover the coast, with overall responsibility held by the North China Sea Fleet (NSF). The North China Sea Fleet Naval Air Force has historically received the most attention of all the PLANAF units, not only because of its proxim-

Operated by the 8th Army Aviation Brigade (38th GA) in Baoding, this Z-10H is well suited for operations in a possible conflict around the Korean peninsula. Its main weapons as shown are KD-10 anti-tank missiles, unguided rockets or PL-90 AAMs. (Top81.cn)

Left: A J-11A operated by the 19th Air Regiment, 7th Fighter Division takes off for a training mission. While overshadowed by new and more modern versions, the type is still an important asset within the PLAAF's fighter fleet and several examples have received an upgrade consisting of new cockpit displays and improved radar.
(FYJS)

Right: A rarely seen J-10A from the 2nd Air Regiment, 1st Fighter Division, based at Chifeng. This division is the PLAAF's premier fighter unit and is currently equipped with three regiments flying J-11B, J-10 and J-8F fighters.
(Top81.cn)

ity to Beijing, but also because of the requirement to defend the strategically important port of Dalian (formerly Port Arthur). More recently, the nearby port of Qingdao became the major base of the PLAN's nuclear attack and ballistic missile submarines, and also houses the HQ of the North China Sea Fleet. According to the latest reports, the aircraft carrier *Liaoning* – even if it may now be officially under the control of the PLN HQ – is assigned to the 1st Destroyer Flotilla just south of Qingdao, close to the Guzhenkou-Wan or Xiangzimen. Since the 1st Flotilla is assigned to the NSF, the *Liaoning* has, at least unofficially, the same assignment. The first carrier air wing of the PLANAF, based with the Naval Aviation Training Base at Huangdicun, is also located in this area.

The PLA is known to have a number of contingency plans in case of a military confrontation on the Korean Peninsula. These were hinted at during the so-called 'August Crisis' of 2015, when North and South Korea almost went to war before the situation was defused through negotiations. During that crisis, Beijing, well known to be usually very restrictive in such cases, intentionally let reports of the deployment of a PLA mechanised brigade to the North Korean border trickle through the internet. Meanwhile, Beijing publicly expressed its concern about the situation on the Korean peninsula and urged both parties to remain calm. Taken together, the response was indicative of the PRC's provision of an 'extra incentive' to smooth negotiations.

The issue of North Korea – and especially that country's ballistic missiles, possibly armed with nuclear warheads – is also one of the greatest importance for South Korea and Japan. There is little doubt that the armed forces of the latter two countries are vastly superior to those of North Korea alone. The situation would be even more advantageous if the US were to provide wartime support – which would almost certainly happen in the case of any major military conflict on the Korean peninsula in the foreseeable future.

However, the biggest question in any such scenario is that of the possible involvement of the PRC. Although it is certain that the PLA has plans for different contingencies related to North Korea, the crucial issue is always going to be that of whether Beijing will be willing to fight another conflict like the Korean War of 1950–53. China actually has very few options in the case of a major crisis involving North Korea. One would be a de-facto invasion of the country which would then be run as a sort of 'vassal state'. Some observers of recent joint exercises between the Chinese and Russian militaries have suggested that these are intended to test concepts for precisely such eventualities. In turn, such an action is unlikely to be tolerated by South Korea and

Left: A JJ-7A assigned to the 21st Regiment, 7th Fighter Division at Yangging/Yongning with a rarely used gun pod under its fuselage. This type provides flight training within regular J-7H units and is assigned to the Central Theater Command.
(Top81.cn)

Right: The JZ-8F – also known as the JC-8F – is a dedicated tactical reconnaissance version of the J-8F interceptor. It features a reconfigurable semi-conformal reconnaissance pod under its fuselage. This particular aircraft is assigned to the 46th Regiment, 16th Specialised Division at Shenyang Yu Hung Tun.
(Top81.cn)

the US, and would probably not be tolerated by Japan either. It is not only Beijing that strictly opposes any ideas of a reunification between North and South Korea: there exists a school of thought in South Korea that the prospect of a unified and economically resurgent Korea would spell disaster for Japan. Therefore, it is alleged, Japan has a vested interest in helping keep the peninsula divided by ensuring Pyongyang's economic survival. For the PRC, status quo is therefore the best available option: this serves to neutralise the economic and military threat of a unified Korea; it keeps Seoul and Pyongyang engaged in a perpetual military standoff; and even ensures that Japan is kept distracted.

The situation is less clear in regard to the latest developments in the ECS. In reaction to earlier claims by Japan and South Korea, Beijing suddenly announced the establishment of its own ADIZ over a wide area of the ECS in November 2013. The newly declared Chinese ADIZ covers the Japanese-claimed Senkaku Islands. The day after Beijing declared the ADIZ, the area was patrolled by one Tu-154M/D (Type II) and a Y-8CB (GX-2) electronic warfare aircraft, both of which were intercepted by Japanese F-15J fighters.

The clearest sign of non-compliance with the Chinese ADIZ was the deployment of US Navy P-3C and EP-3 surveillance aircraft in the same area, and above all a flight by two unarmed USAF B-52H bombers from Anderson Air Force Base on Guam, which transited directly over the disputed island chain without previous notice to Beijing. In advance, US officials had promised that they would challenge the zone. As a result, not only has the PLAAF intensified its operations, but also the PLAN deployed the aircraft carrier *Liaoning* – escorted by two destroyers and two frigates – for a brief cruise in the area.

Taken alone, Beijing's decision was neither particularly unusual nor a provocative act: a number of similar zones exist around the world, including those maintained by Japan, South Korea, Taiwan and the US. All of them extend well beyond the 12nm limit of national sovereign airspace. Indeed, while establishment of the Chinese ADIZ and its overlapping with that of Japan and South Korea caused much uproar outside China, and especially in the West, it seems that most observers have conveniently ignored the fact that the Japanese and South Korean ADIZs over the ECS also overlap. An ADIZ is not a claim of sovereignty and not equivalent to a 'no-fly zone'; it is a security measure: it means that all aircraft entering such a zone are closely monitored and will be intercepted if they fail to comply with the rules imposed by the power that declared the ADIZ.

The Q-5L is a major upgrade of the older Q-5C that finally fulfils the PLAAF's requirement to deliver laser-guided bombs. It features a laser spot tracker under the nose and a K/PZS01H pod to designate the LS-500J. This aircraft is from the 13rd Regiment assigned to the 5th Ground-Attack Division, Weifang-Weixian. (Top81.cn)

Nevertheless, Beijing's announcement prompted a strong reaction not only from Washington, but also from Tokyo. For most of the last 20 years, it was above all the prospect of a nuclear-armed North Korea – possibly supported by the PRC – attacking Japan that represented one of the 'worst case' scenarios for the Japanese armed forces. Meanwhile, PLA activity in the ECS is the primary reason behind the Japanese armed forces flexing their muscles. Therefore, ever since Beijing's declaration of an ADIZ over the ECS, Japan has patrolled its own ADIZ with E-767 AEW&C aircraft, P-3Cs and F-15s, while the US Navy has deployed P-3Cs and EP-3s.

In summary, the threat of an open military conflict in this part of the world is low. As long as all parties involved act responsibly and with mutual understanding and respect, the ADIZs over the East China Sea will remain exactly what they are: mere declarations on paper. However, there remains a concern that at some point one of the parties might misinterpret the intentions or actions of another party. This could result in a serious escalation of territorial disputes.

Left: A JH-7A operated by the 14th Air Regiment, 5th Naval Aviation Division carrying both the type's standard long-range air-to-surface missiles: a KD-88 land attack cruise missile on the inner pylon – plus associated guidance pod – and a YJ-83K anti-ship missile in the middle. (Top81.cn)

Right: The JH-7A was the first aircraft in PLAAF service to use the heavy LS-500J laser-guided bomb in conjunction with the K/JDC01 laser designation pod. This particular aircraft is assigned to the 31st Air Regiment, 11th Ground-Attack Division at Siping. (mil.cnr.cn)

Northern Theater Command

PLAAF aviation units assigned to the Northern Theater Command
(Successor to the former Shenyang MRAF and Jinan MRAF)

Code	Unit (division/regiment)	Base	Aircraft type	Remarks
	1st Fighter Division			HQ Anshan
10x2x (01-49)	1st Air Regiment	Anshan	J-11B/BS	Using older AL-31F instead of WS-10A engines
10x2x (50-99)	2nd Air Regiment	Chifeng	J-10A/AS	Reportedly to receive J-10B or J-10C
11x2x (01-49)	3rd Air Regiment	Anshan	J-8F, JJ-7A	
	5th Ground-Attack Division			HQ Weifang-Weixian
10x6x (01-49)	13th Air Regiment	Weifang-Weixian	Q-5L/J	Base also known as Linyi/Weifang
10x6x (51-99)	14th Air Regiment	Zhucheng	Q-5C/L	
11x6x (01-49)	15th Air Regiment	Weifang-Weixian	JH-7A	
	11th Ground-Attack Division			HQ Siping
20x2x (01-49)	31st Air Regiment	Siping	JH-7A	
20x2x (50-99)	32nd Air Regiment	Dalian Sanshilipu	Q-5	
21x2x (01-49)	33rd Air Regiment	Gongzhuling Huaide	Q-5, Q-5J	
	12th Fighter Division			HQ Jinan
20x3x (01-49)	34th Air Regiment	Qihe	J-10A/AS	
20x3x (51-99)	35th Air Regiment	Gaomi	J-8II, JJ-7	Reportedly to receive J-10A or J-10B
20x3x (01-49)	36th Air Regiment	Wendeng	J-7G, JJ-7A	
	16th Specialised Division			HQ Shenyang Dongta; Base also known as Shenyang-Yuhong
20x7x (01-49)	46th Air Regiment	Shenyang Yu Hung Tun	JZ-8F, JJ-7A	
20x7x (51-99)	47th Air Regiment	Shenyang Yu Hung Tun	Y-8C, Y-8CB (GX-1), Y-8G (GX-4)	
21x7x (01-99)	48th Air Regiment	Shenyang Dongta	Y-7-100	
21x7x (01-99)	48th Air Regiment (det)	Tongxian	Y-5, Y-7, Z-9WZ	
	19th Fighter Division			HQ Jining
30x0x (01-49)	55th Air Regiment	Jining	J-11, Su-27SK/UBK	
30x0x (50-99)	56th Air Regiment	Zhengzhou	J-7B, JJ-7	Reportedly to receive J-10B
31x0x (01-49)	57th Air Regiment	Shangqiu (Zhuji Guanyintang)	J-7H, JJ-7	
	21st Fighter Division	HQ Qiqihar		
30x2x (01-49)	61st Air Regiment	Yanji	J-7E, JJ-7A	Reportedly to receive J-10A/AS
30x2x (51-99)	62nd Air Regiment	Qiqihar	J-8DH/H/F, JJ-7A	Base also known as Qiqihar-Sanjiazi
31x2x (01-49)	63rd Air Regiment	Mudanjiang-Hailang	J-7H, JJ-7A	
	32nd Fighter Division			HQ Lianyungang, Baitabu
40x3x (01-49)	94th Air Regiment	Xuzhou/Daguozhuang	J-7B, JJ-7A	
40x3x (51-99)	95th Air Regiment	Lianyungang, Baitabu	J-11B/BS	
41x3x (01-49)	96th Air Regiment	Xintai	Y-5, Y-7, Z-9B	

	Dalian Base			HQ Dandong
69x9x (01-49)	88th Brigade	Dandong/Langtou	J-7E	
70x0x (01-49)	89th Brigade	Pulandian	J-11B/BS	
70x1x (01-49)	90th Brigade	Wafangdian	Q-5B, JJ-6	
70x2x (01-49)	91st Brigade	Liuhe	J-7H	

Forward operating base at Hailar/Southwest

Northern Theater Command

PLANAF units assigned to the Northern Theater Command Navy
(Successor to the North China Sea Fleet Naval Air Force)

Code	Unit (division/regiment)	Base	Aircraft type	Remarks
	2nd Naval Aviation Division (Specialised)			HQ Laiyang
9xx1	4th Air Regiment	Laiyang	Y-8J, Y-8W (GX-5)	AEW&C unit
9xx3	5th Air Regiment (det)	Qingdao-Tuandao	SH-5	ASW unit; to be replaced by Y-9Q (GX-6) in 2016
9xx6	5th Air Regiment	Qingdao-Licang	SA321Ja, Z-8JH, Z-9C/D, Y-5	Also known as Changkou Naval Air Station
9xx1	6th Air Regiment	Dalian-Tuchengzi	Y-8X, Y-8JB (GX-2), Y-9JB (GX-8)	EW/ELINT/SIGINT unit
	5th Naval Aviation Division			HQ Yantai-Laishan
82x7x	13th Air Regiment	Shanhaiguan	JH-7A	Also known as Qinhuangdao Naval Air Station; former 7th Division, not yet renumbered
82x5x	14th Air Regiment	Yantai-Laishan	JH-7A	
83x5x	15th Air Regiment	Jiaozhou	J-8F/FH, JZ-8F, JL-9H	Dispersal at Qingdao-Liuting

PLANAF units directly assigned to PLAN Headquarters

	Carrier Air Wing Base			
1xx	Detachment or new unit	Huangdicun	J-15	Also known as Xingcheng-2; types are temporarily assigned on board *Liaoning* (CV-16)
xxx			Z-18 (VIP), Z-18F (ASW), Z-18J/YJ (AEW)	
37x			Z-9C/D (SAR)	

▶▶ Map of the Northern Theater Command for PLAAF and PLANAF and the Central Theater Command for PLAAF. (Map by James Lawrence)

Central Theater Command

PLAAF aviation units assigned to the Central Theater Command

(Successor to the former Beijing MRAF)

Code	Unit (division/regiment)	Base	Aircraft type	Remarks
	7th Fighter Division			HQ Zhangjiakou
10x8x (01-49)	19th Air Regiment	Zhangjiakou	J-11, J-11BS Su-27SK/UBK	
10x8x (51-99)	20th Air Regiment	Tangshan	J-7B, JJ-7A	
11x8x (01-50)	21st Air Regiment	Yangging/Yongning	J-7B, JJ-7A	
	15th Ground-Attack Division			HQ Datong-Huairen
20x6x (01-49)	43rd Air Regiment	Datong-Huairen	J-10A/AS	
20x6x (50-99)	44th Air Regiment	Hohhot-Bikeqi	J-7G, JJ-7A	
21x6x (01-52)	45th Air Regiment	Qizhou-Dingxian	Q-5B/C/L/J	
	24th Fighter Division			HQ Tianjin Yangcun
30x5x (01-49)	70th Air Regiment	Zunhua	J-7G, JJ-7A	
30x5x (51-99)	72nd Air Regiment	Tianjin Yangcun	J-10A/AS	
0x 1x	Ba Yi (1 August) Aerial Demonstration Team	Tainjin Yangcun	J-10AY, J-10SY	
	36th Bomber Division			HQ Lintong
98x 87x 60xx	106th Aerial Survey Regiment	Hanzhong-Chenggu	Y-8H An-30 Y-12IV	Status unclear
40x7x (01-49)	107th Air Regiment	Lintong	H-6H	Status unclear; base also known as Xi'an/Lintong
40x7x (51-99)	108th Air Regiment	Wugong	H-6H/M	

Forward operating bases at Baoji and Xishanbeixiang (Tong Lin Chuan)

Aviation units directly assigned to the PLAAF Headquarters/Central Command

Code	Unit (division/regiment)	Base	Aircraft type	Remarks
	34th Transport Division			HQ Beijing-Nanyuan – unit reports directly to PLAAF HQ
B-401x B-406x B-409x B-400x B-402x B-408x	100th Air Regiment (det)	Beijing/Xijiao	CRJ-200BLR CRJ-700 A319-115 ACJ 737-300 737-700 737-800	
21xx	100th Air Regiment	Beijing/Shahezhen	EC225, AS332L-1	
B-407x B-601x	101st Air Regiment	Xingtai-Shahe	Y-7 Y-7G	Location uncertain, may also be at Shahe (Hebei)
B-401x B-405x B-408x	102nd Air Regiment	Beijing-Nanyuan	Tu-154M/D 737-3Q8 Learjet 35A/36A	
6x1x 6x2x	203rd Air Regiment	Beijing/Shahezhen	Z-9B Y-5, Y-7	Also known as Shahe
	Strategic UAV Scouting Force			
?	Unknown UAV unit	Close to Shahe	CJ-6, BZK-005 BZK-009 (?)	Directly subordinated to the PLA General Staff Department

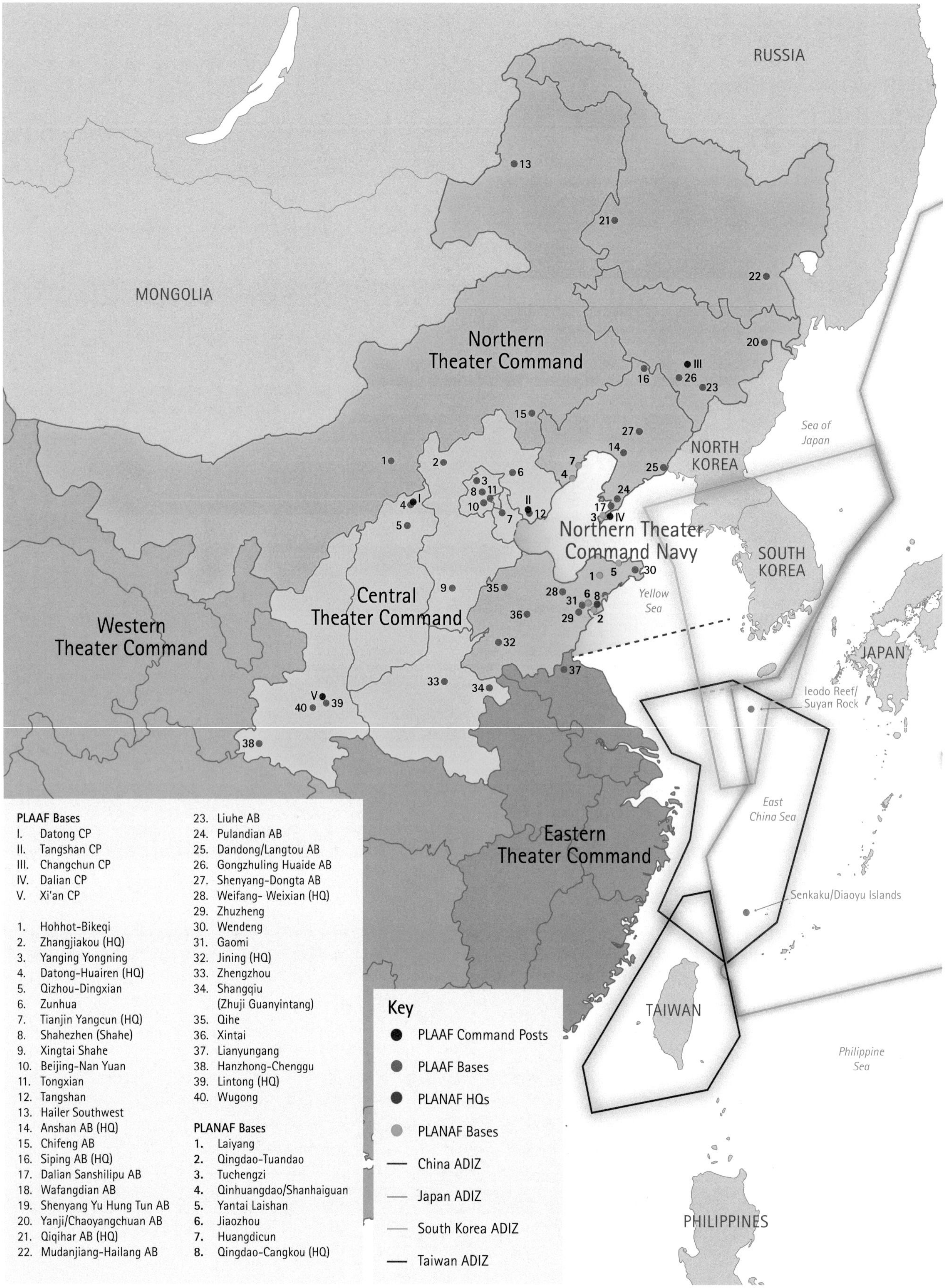
RUSSIA
MONGOLIA
Northern Theater Command
Western Theater Command
Central Theater Command
Eastern Theater Command
Northern Theater Command Navy
NORTH KOREA
SOUTH KOREA
JAPAN
TAIWAN
PHILIPPINES
Sea of Japan
Yellow Sea
East China Sea
Philippine Sea
Ieodo Reef/ Suyan Rock
Senkaku/Diaoyu Islands
PLAAF Bases
I. Datong CP
II. Tangshan CP
III. Changchun CP
IV. Dalian CP
V. Xi'an CP
1. Hohhot-Bikeqi
2. Zhangjiakou (HQ)
3. Yanging Yongning
4. Datong-Huairen (HQ)
5. Qizhou-Dingxian
6. Zunhua
7. Tianjin Yangcun (HQ)
8. Shahezhen (Shahe)
9. Xingtai Shahe
10. Beijing-Nan Yuan
11. Tongxian
12. Tangshan
13. Hailer Southwest
14. Anshan AB (HQ)
15. Chifeng AB
16. Siping AB (HQ)
17. Dalian Sanshilipu AB
18. Wafangdian AB
19. Shenyang Yu Hung Tun AB
20. Yanji/Chaoyangchuan AB
21. Qiqihar AB (HQ)
22. Mudanjiang-Hailang AB
23. Liuhe AB
24. Pulandian AB
25. Dandong/Langtou AB
26. Gongzhuling Huaide AB
27. Shenyang-Dongta AB
28. Weifang- Weixian (HQ)
29. Zhuzheng
30. Wendeng
31. Gaomi
32. Jining (HQ)
33. Zhengzhou
34. Shangqiu (Zhuji Guanyintang)
35. Qihe
36. Xintai
37. Lianyungang
38. Hanzhong-Chenggu
39. Lintong (HQ)
40. Wugong
PLANAF Bases
1. Laiyang
2. Qingdao-Tuandao
3. Tuchengzi
4. Qinhuangdao/Shanhaiguan
5. Yantai Laishan
6. Jiaozhou
7. Huangdicun
8. Qingdao-Cangkou (HQ)
Key
PLAAF Command Posts
PLAAF Bases
PLANAF HQs
PLANAF Bases
China ADIZ
Japan ADIZ
South Korea ADIZ
Taiwan ADIZ

EASTERN THEATER COMMAND

The issue of Taiwan is a very special one for the PRC, and certainly the top priority in regard to the PLA's modernisation drive. This is clearly indicated by the official order of protocol, which lists the responsible Eastern Theater Command first. This fact is repeatedly mentioned in the most relevant official publications released by Beijing, including the recently published 'Chinese Military Strategy':

'The Taiwan issue bears on China's reunification and long-term development, and reunification is an inevitable trend in the course of national rejuvenation. In recent years, cross-Taiwan Strait relations have sustained a sound momentum of peaceful development, but the root cause of instability has not yet been removed, and the 'Taiwan independence' separatist forces and their activities are still the biggest threat to the peaceful development of cross-Strait relations.'

Taiwan

An indigenous AIDC F-CK-1C Ching-Kuo from the RoC's 1st TFW/9th TFG based at Tainan. The fighter is armed with two (wingtip) TC-1 Sky Sword and one TC-2 Sky Sword II AAMs. (Gilles Denis)

Taiwan (formerly known as Formosa) is an island located about 180km (112 miles) off the southeastern coast of China, adjacent to Fujian Province. Inhabited by Taiwanese Aborigines in ancient times, it came under the control of the Han Chinese in the 17th century. Following a brief phase of independence, it slipped under the control of the Qing Dynasty in 1683, and was considered an outlying prefecture of Fujian Province until 1887, when it became a separate province, before being annexed by Japan after the First Sino-Japanese War of 1895.

In 1912, the Republic of China (RoC) was established in mainland China under the so-called Nationalist (or Kuomintang) government, which was considered one of five major allies against the Axis forces during the World War II. Following Japan's capitulation in 1945, the RoC gained control of Taiwan, although this was still officially Japanese territory. After losing the Chinese Civil War in May 1950, the Kuomintang government withdrew to Taiwan and Japan formally renounced all territorial rights upon the island in the San Francisco Peace Treaty of 1952.

Meanwhile, the Communist Party of China took full control of mainland China and founded the PRC, and the RoC thus began functioning as a quasi government in exile. Nevertheless, the RoC government continued to represent China, even in the UN until October 1971, when its responsibilities there were assumed by the PRC. Ever since, international recognition of the RoC as the sole representative of China has gradually eroded: indeed, most UN members have switched their recognition to the PRC.

Left: RoCAF F-16A serial number 6699 from the 4th TFW/23rd TFG based at Chiayi with a full load of weapons: four AIM-9M Sidewinders, two AIM-7M Sparrows and an AN/ALQ-184 countermeasures pod. (Gilles Denis)

Right: All Taiwanese Mirage 2000-5s serve with the 2nd TFW, based at Hsinchu. Mirage 2000-5DI serial number 2061 is seen here during a highway landing exercise. (Lin Yu-Chun)

Since 1950, all relations between the two countries – commonly designated 'cross-Strait relations' – have been undertaken between the two respective governments of China, neither of which considers the other as legitimate. Not surprisingly, their relations through much of the 1950s and 1960s were characterised by continued, low-scale military conflicts.

Officially, the PRC and Taiwan do not maintain any direct and official relations. Because each government considers itself the sole legitimate representative of the same state, and they share the perception that China and Taiwan are parts of the same state, neither sees their relations as 'foreign' relations. Nevertheless, there are regular negotiations via intermediaries including the Association for Relations Across the Taiwan Strait in the PRC and the Strait Exchange Foundation in Taiwan.

In the 1980s, the government of the PRC proposed to Taiwan a solution similar to what it had done in the case of Hong Kong and Macau, the so-called 'One Country, Two Systems' principle of governance. In this system, these distinct Chinese regions retain their own, 'capitalist' economic and political systems and maintain all legal, economic and financial affairs, including external relations with foreign countries, while the rest of the PRC retains the socialist system. With the aim of maintaining good relations with the US, Beijing even suggested allowing Taiwan near-complete autonomy, including the right to maintain its own military. The government of Taiwan rejected this proposal and instead opted for a closer relationship to Washington, which repeatedly issued special security guarantees for the island. According to the latest of these, the Taiwan Relations Act from 1982, the US is not only obliged to intervene militarily if the PRC attacks or invades Taiwan, but also to make available to the local government such defence articles and services as might be necessary to enable it to maintain a sufficient self-defence capabilities. This US policy of 'strategic ambiguity' had two goals in mind: it aimed to prevent any kind of unilateral steps made by the PRC against Taiwan, but also dissuaded Taiwan from a unilateral declaration of independence.

During the last 20 years, the PRC and Taiwan have established close economic relations, which have not only resulted in intensive cooperation but also in the first official meeting between representatives of both governments, in Nanjing in February 2014. However, aside from regular negotiations related to the expansion of the so-called 'three links' (transportation, commerce, communications), there has been relatively little progress in terms of a political plan. On the contrary, there are fundamental differences between Beijing and Taipei: the former insists that the government of the PRC is the only legitimate government of China and refers to the government in Taipei only as the 'Taiwan Authority', while the latter increasingly sees itself as a sovereign state, with its own constitution and elected democratic government, modern industrialised economy, and its own armed forces.

Capabilities and intentions: East and Southeast Asia

There is little doubt that one of the primary goals of the Chinese military modernisation effort is to develop military options for addressing the situation in regard to Taiwan; indeed, this is one of the primary missions of the entire PLA. Although tensions here have significantly decreased in recent years, and although China and Taiwan have reached 18 agreements for cross-Strait cooperation on cultural, economic and functional issues, official Beijing still considers Taiwan as part of the PRC, a 'renegade' province. Despite occasional signs of impatience, China appears content to respect Taiwan's current approach to cross-Strait relations: nevertheless, the PLA has developed and deployed military capabilities to coerce Taiwan or even attempt an invasion.

Following the latest restructuring, the primary importance of today's Eastern Theater Command – de facto the former Nanjing MR – lies in its proximity to Taiwan. Meanwhile, the adjacent Southern Theater Command (see Chapter 4) acts as a backup in case of a crisis, similar to the former Guangzhou MR. Usually, their primary responsibility remains air defence of the eastern provinces and the city of Shanghai. However, this area includes a significant number of major bases for PLA ground forces and missile units.

In recent years the PLAAF has significantly reinforced local units through the introduction to service of types including the J-11A, Su-30MKK and JH-7A, a division equipped with the latest H-6K bombers, and support platforms based on the Y-8 transport. The availability of all these assets and their much improved training not only point to the importance of this command but also make this air arm capable of saturating Taiwan with superior numbers of aircraft of at least equal capabilities.

The 14th Fighter Division is the only PLAAF division that fields two J-11 regiments: this particular aircraft is assigned to the 40th Regiment at Nanchang-Xiangtang, whereas the 41st Regiment is based at Wuyishan. Both units operate older J-11A models. (FYJS)

Two J-10AHs from the 12th Regiment, 4th Naval Aviation Division at Huangyan/Luqiao take on fuel from an H-6DU tanker of the 23rd Regiment, 8th Naval Aviation Division assigned to the Southern Theater Command. (meyet.cn)

The branch of the PLANAF opposing Taiwan is the Eastern Theater Command Navy – successor to the former East Sea Fleet – the responsibility of which extends from the Shandong/Jaingsu provincial border to the Fujian/Guangdong provincial border. PLANAF units of this command are primarily equipped for anti-ship and ground-attack purposes, and – among others – include a regiment each of H-6 bombers and Su-30MKK strike aircraft, and two regiments of JH-7 fighter-bombers.

A unique and little-understood unit is a brigade equipped with retired J-6 fighters converted to become J-6W/B-6 unmanned combat aerial vehicles (UCAVs). These are intended to act as decoys to probe, disrupt or even suppress enemy air defence systems. The first PLANAF unmanned aerial vehicle (UAV) unit has also been based in this area since 2010, and is equipped with BZK-005Hs.

Not surprisingly considering this concentration of PLA forces, even in peacetime the situation in the skies over the Taiwan Strait has experienced dramatic change over the last 20 years. The units of the Eastern Theater Command are now actively seeking to limit the freedom of action previously enjoyed in the area by the Republic of China Air Force (RoCAF). In earlier times, Taiwanese combat and reconnaissance aircraft were capable of operating at least as far as the middle of the Strait.

Today, Taiwanese F-16s equipped for reconnaissance are locked on by multiple PLAAF interceptors even as they climb out from their home bases. Indicating a constant alert status and very high readiness rates on the part of the Chinese air arms, such actions prevent the RoCAF from gathering even a bare minimum of intelligence concerning PLAAF and PLANAF activity. As well as blocking operations against the

The rarely seen Y-8GX-4 – or Y-8T – was long thought to carry the GX-3 designation. Assigned to the 26th Special Mission Division, this example is taking off from Wuxi-Shuofang. This airborne command post was the last special missions type to be based on the old Y-8 airframe. Today four Y-8Ts are operational, all facing Taiwan. (Top81.cn)

The Y-8GX-3 – or Y-8G – was long thought to have the GX-4 designation. This electronic warfare type features two huge 'hamster cheeks' containing antennas for long-range electronic/communication jamming missions. Eight Y-8Gs are operational within the 20th Division facing India and Vietnam and, as seen here, with the 10th Bomber Division facing Taiwan. (Top81.cn)

The KJ-500 – also known as the Y-8GX-10 – became China's latest AEW&C type when it entered service with both the PLAAF and PLANAF in early 2015. In this role, it supersedes the earlier KJ-200 and supplements the larger KJ-2000. (Top81.cn)

The latest member of the H-6 family is the H-6K featuring a completely revised airframe and Russian D-30KP-2 turbofan engines replacing the inefficient WP-8/AM-3 turbojets. Its main weapon is the KD-20 long-range cruise missile. Two regiments are equipped with this type, both facing Taiwan. (Top.81.cn)

RoCAF, the PLAAF routinely operates with large formations of combat aircraft over the Taiwan Strait, including fighters and interceptors of different types, supported by tankers and AEW&C aircraft.

Although they often approach the middle of the Strait, the Chinese aircraft never cross an imaginary line running down the crucial waterway. Nevertheless, this is a dramatic development considering that, historically, Taiwan's security has been primarily based upon the PLA's inability to project power across the Taiwan Strait to overcome the natural geographic advantages of island defence, as well as Taiwan's superiority in terms of military technology.

While the PRC appears ready to defer the use of force against Taiwan – at least as long as it believes that unification over the long term remains possible (and as long as the costs of conflict outweigh the benefits) – Beijing has made it obvious that the credible threat of force is essential to maintain the conditions for political progress, and to prevent Taiwan from declaring de jure independence. Indeed, after nearly a decade of relative calm, the landslide election of an independence-leaning opposition leader in Taiwan has put that country back into the spotlight as one of Asia's major powder kegs.

Eastern Theater Command

PLAAF aviation units assigned to the Eastern Theater Command
(Successor to the former Nanjing MRAF)

Code	Unit (division/regiment)	Base	Aircraft type	Remarks
	3rd Fighter Division			HQ Wuhu
10x4x (01-49)	7th Air Regiment	Wuhu	J-7E, JJ-7A	Reportedly under conversion to J-16
10x4x (51-99)	8th Air Regiment	Changxing	J-10A/AS	
11x4x (01-49)	9th Air Regiment	Wuhu	Su-30MKK	
	10th Bomber Division			HQ Anqing
20x1x (01-49)	28th Air Regiment	Anqing North or Liuhe	H-6K	
20x1x (51-99)	29th Air Regiment	Luhe/Ma'an	H-6H, Y-8T (GX-4)	
21x1x (01-49)	30th Electronic Warfare Regiment	Luhe/Ma'an (unc.)	Y-8C, Y-8CB (GX-1), Y-8G (GX-3), Y-8XZ (GX-7)	
	14th Fighter Division			HQ Nanchang-Xiangtang
20x5x (01-49)	40th Air Regiment	Nanchang-Xiangtang	J-11A, Su-27UBK	
20x5x (51-55)	41st Air Regiment	Wuyishan	J-11A, Su-27UBK	
21x5x (01-49)	42nd Air Regiment	Zhangshu	J-7E	
	26th Special Mission Division			HQ Wuxi-Shuofang
3007x 3017x 3027x 3037x 3047x	76th Airborne Command and Control Regiment	Wuxi-Shuofang	KJ-2000, KJ-200 (GX-5), Y-8T (GX-4), Y-8C, KJ-500 (GX-10)	
30x7x (51-99)	77th Air Regiment	Nanjing-Daiiaochang	Y-7-100, Y-7G	Base also known as Daxiao
30x7x (51-99)	77th Air Regiment – (SAR det)	Nanjing	Z-8KA, Mi-171, Y-5	
	28th Ground-Attack Division			HQ Hangzhou-Jinqiao
30x9x (01-49)	82nd Air Regiment	Hangzhou-Jianqiao	Q-5D/J	
30x9x (51-99)	83rd Air Regiment	Hangzhou-Jianqiao	JH-7A	
31x9x (01-49)	84th Air Regiment	Jiaxing	JH-7A	
	Shanghai Base			HQ Quzhou
68x9x (01-49)	78th Brigade	Shanghai-Chongming Island	J-8DH, JJ-7A	
69x6x (01-49)	85th Brigade	Quzhou	Su-30MKK	
69x7x (01-49)	86th Brigade	Rugao	J-7E, JJ-7A	
70x4x (01-49)	93rd Brigade	Suzhou	JZ-8F, JJ-7A	Base also known as Suzhou-Guangfu
	180th Unmanned Attack Brigade			HQ unknown
?	1st Dadui	Liangcheng Longyan Guanzhi	J-6W/B-6 UCAV	Also forward operating base
?	2nd Dadui	Yangtang Li	J-6W/B-6 UCAV	Located in the Guangshou MR/ Southern Theater Command
?	3rd Dadui	Wuyishan	J-6W/B-6 UCAV	

?	4th Dadui	Ji-an/Taihe Liancheng	J-6W/B-6 UCAV	Also known as Jinggangshan
?	5th Dadui	Fuzhou	J-6W/B-6 UCAV	
	Note: The organisational structure of this unit is unclear since it consists of several sub-units (Fendui) dispersed over different airfields. Sub-units identified to date are: 60F = Xingning, 61F = Liangcheng, 70F = Wuyishan, 71F = Jinjiang (Quanzhou-Jinjiang), 75F = Hui'an (Luocheng/Huian), 80F = Longtian (also forward operating base), and 85F = Fuzhou			
	UAV Division			
?	1st UAV Battalion	Ningbo/Zhuangqiao	BZK-005	
?	2nd UAV Battalion	Daishan	BZK-005 BZK-007	

Forward operating bases at Luocheng/Huian, Xiapu and Zhangzhou

Aviation units directly assigned to the PLAAF Headquarters/Central Command

Code	Unit (division/regiment)	Base	Aircraft type	Remarks
	15th Airborne Army			HQ Xiaogan; former 15th Airborne Corps
2xx4x (001-049)	43rd Airborne Division	Kaifeng	Y-8C	127th, 128th and 129th Airborne Regiments
6x5x	6th Transport Regiment (det)	Yingshan/ North Guangshui	Y-5, Y-7, Y-8 Y-12IV	
6x5x	6th Transport Regiment	Xiaogan	Y-5, Y-7, Y-8	
6x6x	Independent Helicopter Wing/Dadui	Huangpi	Z-8KA, Z-9WE/WZ Z-10K	

Seen here during the 2015 Victory Parade 2015 celebrating the end of World War II, the BZK-005 'Giant Eagle' was China's first HALE-type reconnaissance UAV and is now operational within the PLAAF, PLANAF and the PLA General Staff Department. Seen behind is a smaller tactical BZK-006 (or WZ-6) tactical UAV used by the PLA Army. (Top81.cn)

Eastern Theater Command

PLANAF units assigned to the Eastern Theater Command Navy

(Successor to the for East China Sea Fleet Naval Air Force)

Code	Unit (division/regiment)	Base	Aircraft type	Remarks
	4th Naval Aviation Division			HQ Ningbo-Zhuangqiao
81x4x	10th Air Regiment	Feidong	Su-30MK2	
9xx4	11th Air Regiment	Ningbo-Zhuangqiao	Mi-8, Ka-28, Ka-31	Former 4th Independent Regiment, not yet renumbered
83x4x	12th Air Regiment	Huangyan/ Luqiao (Taizhou)	J-10AH, J-10ASH	
	6th Naval Aviation Division			HQ Shanghai-Dachang
81x6x	16th Air Regiment	Shanghai-Dachang	JH-7 (Batch 01 mod.)	
81x1x	17th Air Regiment	Jiangsu Benniu	H-6G, + a few H-6A	Former 1st AR/1st BD, not yet renumbered; base also known as Changzhou NAS
82x6x	18th Air Regiment	Yiwu	JH-7 (Batch 02)	
HY-0x	Reconnaissance Dadui	Huangyan/ Luqiao (Taizhou)	BZK-005H UAV	

A Su-30MK2 operated by the 10th Regiment, 4th Naval Aviation Division at Feidong. This type was ordered in 2003 and features an upgraded N001VEP radar. Usually a strike aircraft, the type is also used as a long-range interceptor over the East China Sea. (FYJS)

This JH-7 is one of the few Batch 02 aircraft that equip the 18th Regiment within the 6th Naval Aviation Division at Yiwu. The same division also operates a second regiment at Dachang equipped with the older JH-7 Batch 01 but modified to the same standard. Both are usually seen operating over the East China Sea. (Top81.cn)

PLAAF Bases

I. Fuzhou CP
II. Shanghai CP
III. Zhangzhou CP

1. Wuhu (HQ)
2. Changxing
3. Anqing North (HQ)
4. Nanjing-Dajiaochang
5. Nanchang-Xiangtang (HQ)
6. Wuyishan
7. Zhangshu
8. Wuxi-Shuofang
9. Nanjing-Tushan
10. Hangzhou-Jianqiao
11. Jiaxing
12. Luhe/Ma'an
13. Daishan
14. Quzho
15. Rugao
16. Shanghai-Chongmin
17. Suzhou
18. Liangcheng Longyan Guanzhi
19. Ji-an/Taihe Liancheng
20. Fuzhou
21. Luocheng/Huian
22. Ningbo/Zhuangqiao
23. Longtian
24. Zhangzhou
25. Xiapu

PLANAF Bases

IV. Ningbo-Zhuangqiao HQ

26. Feidong
27. Huangyan/Luqiao
28. Shanghai-Dachang
29. Changzhou/Benniu
30. Yiwu

Key

- PLAAF Command Posts
- PLAAF Bases
- PLANAF HQs
- PLANAF Bases
- China ADIZ
- Taiwan ADIZ

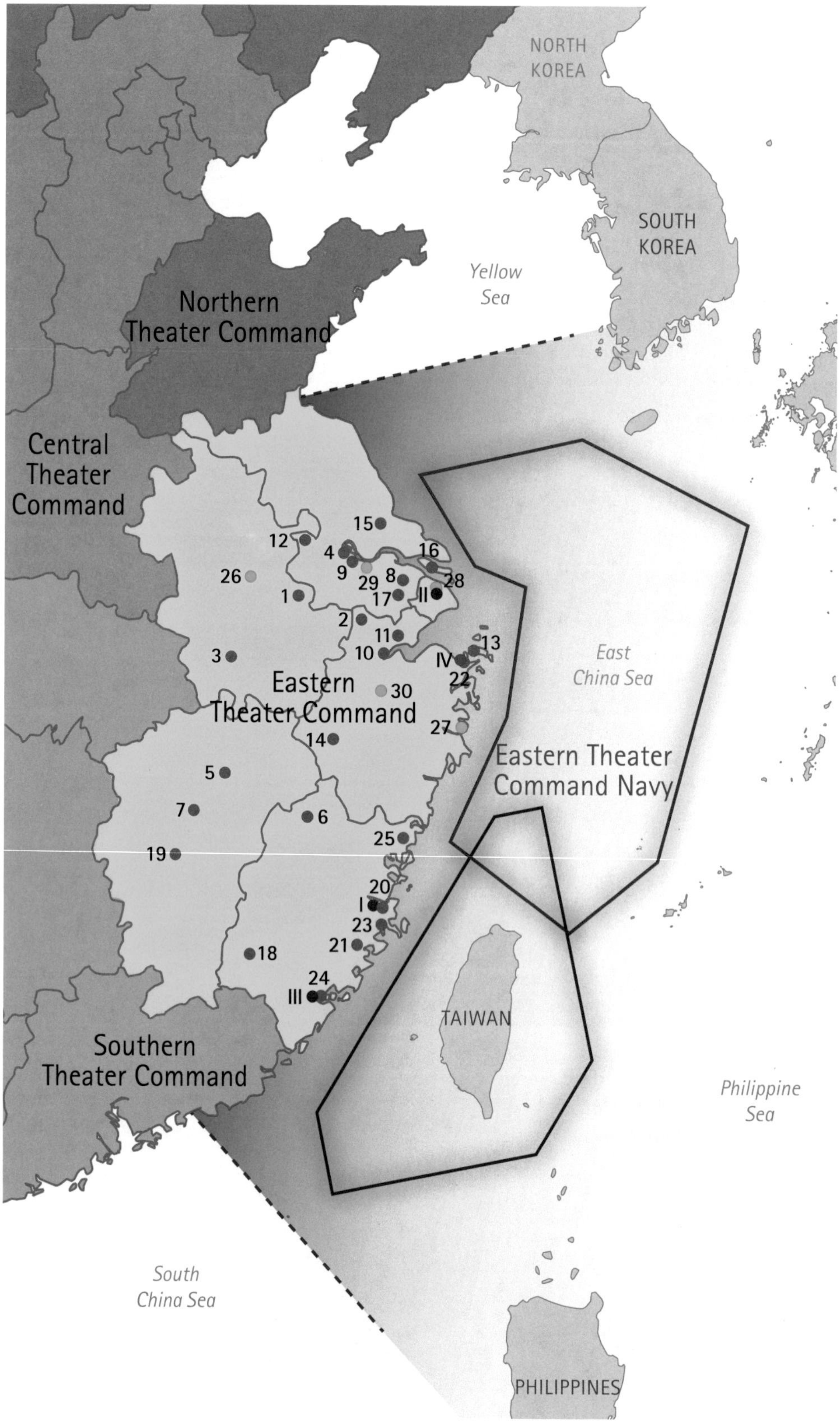

Map of the Eastern Theater Command for PLAAF and PLANAF.
(Map by James Lawrence)

SOUTHERN THEATER COMMAND

Following the PLA's reorganisation, the Southern Theater Command – in fact, the successor to the Guangzhou MR – has been responsible for air defence of the southern provinces including the Hong Kong Special Administrative Region and Macau. Akin to the former Guangzhou, the Southern Command is the second of two regions facing Taiwan, and strategic importance is added by the fact that it also faces Vietnam and the Philippines, and includes Hong Kong and the flourishing economic zones surrounding it. However, its most important geographical area is surely the South China Sea (SCS) and the issues surrounding the islands there.

In line with the recent structural reform, the geographical structure of this theater command remains the least known, since there are several contradictory reports concerning the assignment of the Yunnan and Guizhou Provinces (formerly Chengdu MR) as well as Hubei Province (it is unclear if this falls under the Central Theater Command or remains in the Southern Theater Command). However, in terms of military issues it makes sense to unite the South Asian countries under this command and separate them from the Himalayan region.

South China Sea

Nowhere else has recent PRC expansion caused as much discussion and even unrest as in the SCS and especially the areas of the Paracel and Spratly Islands, the Pratas Islands, the Macclesfield Bank, and the Scarborough Shoal. The reasons are multiple and range from the acquisition of additional fishing areas (the SCS is assessed as accounting for up to 10 per cent of the world's fish-catch); exploitation of suspected natural resources (including oil and gas); and control over several crucial trade routes between Northeast and Southeast Asia (totalling about 50 per cent of the world's annual merchant fleet tonnage and one third of all maritime traffic). Aside for the PRC, a number of other nations make claims on the areas in question, including Malaysia, the Philippines, Taiwan and Vietnam. Only the PRC, Taiwan and Vietnam base their claims on historical sovereignty, while the Philippines base their claims on the United Nations Convention on the Law of the Sea (UNCLOS) of 2009.

The dispute over the SCS is primarily centred around the claims of maritime boundaries and specific 'territories'. The latter especially are somewhat abstract, since they vary considerably between small islands, rocks, low-tide elevations, underwater reefs, banks, and shoals. Meanwhile, the UNCLOS only clearly distinguishes between three types of feature:

- **Islands:** naturally formed land areas capable of sustaining human habitation or even economic life; entitled to a 12nm radius of territorial waters and 200nm of EEZ;
- **Rocks or high-tide elevations:** areas of land that lie above the waterline even at high tide, but incapable of sustaining human habitation or economic life; these areas can also expand into 12nm of territorial waters, but are not entitled to serve as a basis for an EEZ;
- **Low-tide elevations and sunken reefs:** features that lie below the surface at high tide, which cannot be claimed as national territory, although artificial installations upon them are entitled to a safety zone with a radius of 500m (547yd).

Without entering an in-depth discussion concerning codification and judicial issues, in summary, the majority of parties involved acknowledge the so-called III UNCLOS of 2009 as providing a valid codification for the SCS. Correspondingly, Vietnam claims the northern portion of the SCS including the Paracel Islands; Malaysia claims a sector in the middle of the SCS; Brunei has issued only a preliminary submission that notified the UN of its intention to claim a continental shelf beyond the 200nm limit; and the Philippines considers its claims for much of the northern SCS as valid under the UNCLOS. These parties, and the US – which has so far refused to ratify the UNCLOS but recognises it as a codification of customary international law – insist on maintaining the so-called 'status quo' in the area.

On the contrary, the government of the PRC has never issued any formal claims over the SCS. Instead, and drawing upon sovereignty claims dating from the 1940s, in reaction to the III UNCLOS, the PRC demanded that the UN refuse to consider any claims upon the SCS by other parties, and issued a stern warning to all countries not to claim the islands that the PRC regards as its own sovereign territory.

A cross-examination of Chinese and various UNCLOS-related claims results in the definition of six areas of dispute within the SCS, as follows:

Claims and disputes	Countries involved
Nine-dashed line	Brunei, Cambodia, Indonesia, Malaysia, PRC, Philippines, Singapore, Taiwan, Vietnam
Paracel Islands	PRC, Vietnam, Taiwan
Pratas Islands (also Dongsha Islands)	PRC, Taiwan
Spratly Islands	Brunei, Malaysia, PRC, Philippines, Taiwan, Vietnam
Zhonghsa Islands (also Scarborough Shoal and Macclesfield Bank)	PRC, Philippines, Taiwan
Island reclamation ('Great Wall of Sand') by PRC within Paracels and Spratlys	PRC, Taiwan, Vietnam

Islands Key

- China
- Malaysia
- Philippines
- Taiwan
- Vietnam

--- Claimed by China
--- Claimed by Indonesia
--- Claimed by Malaysia
--- Claimed by Philippines
--- Claimed by Vietnam
--- Claimed by Brunei

▶ A map of the disputed Spratly Islands within the South China Sea showing all claims and the nine-dashed line. (Map by Lames Lawerence)

Nine-dashed line

It is often asserted that China claims sovereignty over almost the entire SCS. Such viewpoints are actually based upon a misunderstanding of the so-called 'nine-dashed line'. In late 1947, the PRC published a map claiming sovereignty over specific 'Islands of the South China Sea and the adjacent waters'. Based on claims originally dating back to the times of the Yuan Dynasty, and repeated by the government of the Republic of China (nowadays Taiwan), the map in question showed a u-shaped line originally

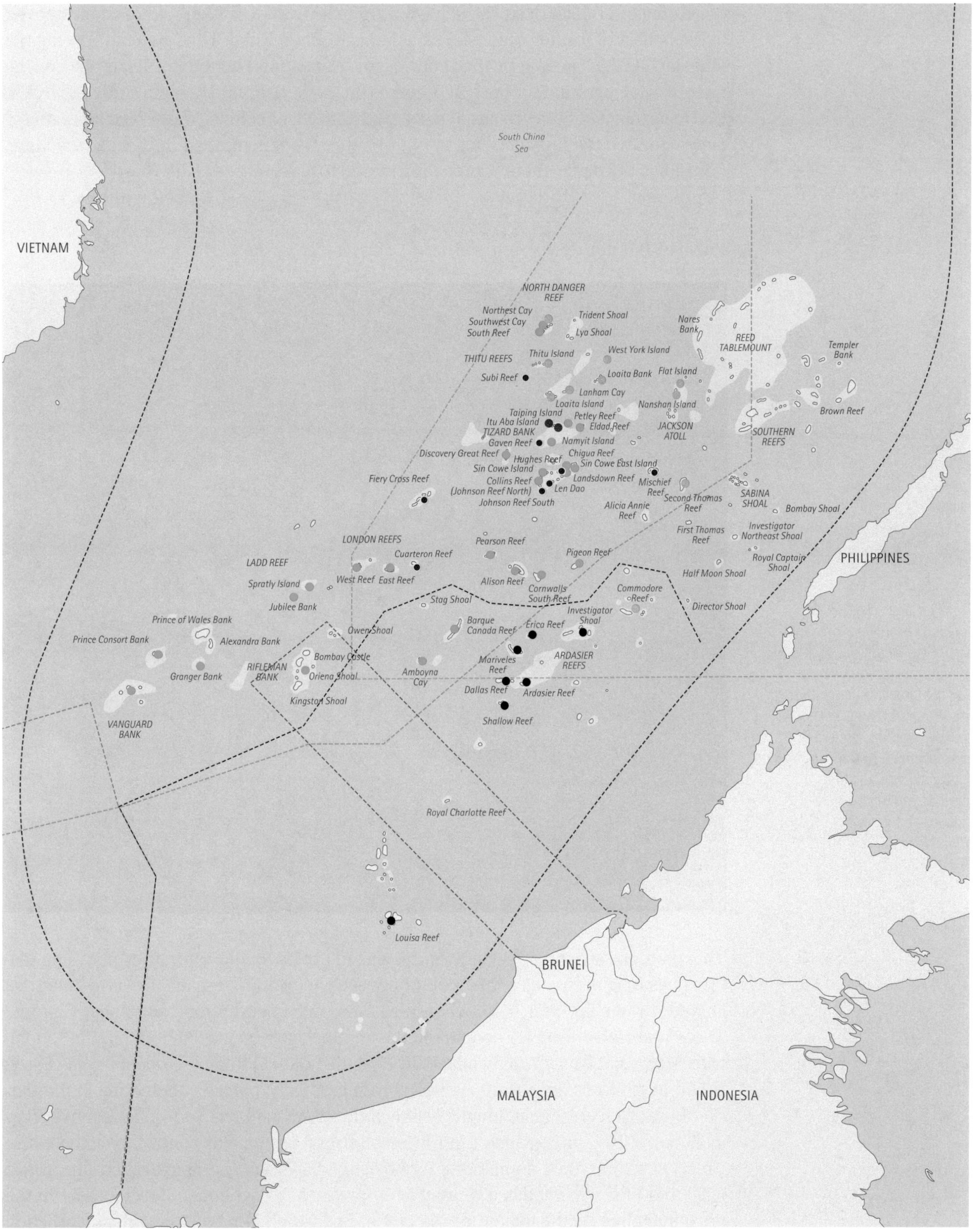
South China Sea
VIETNAM
NORTH DANGER REEF
Northest Cay
Southwest Cay
South Reef
Trident Shoal
Lya Shoal
Nares Bank
REED TABLEMOUNT
Templer Bank
THITU REEFS
Thitu Island
West York Island
Subi Reef
Loaita Bank
Flat Island
Lanham Cay
Loaita Island
Nanshan Island
Brown Reef
Taiping Island
Itu Aba Island
TIZARD BANK
Petley Reef
Eldad Reef
JACKSON ATOLL
SOUTHERN REEFS
Gaven Reef
Namyit Island
Discovery Great Reef
Chigua Reef
Hughes Reef
Sin Cowe East Island
Sin Cowe Island
Landsdown Reef
Fiery Cross Reef
Collins Reef
(Johnson Reef North)
Len Dao
Mischief Reef
Second Thomas Reef
SABINA SHOAL
Bombay Shoal
Johnson Reef South
Alicia Annie Reef
First Thomas Reef
Investigator Northeast Shoal
LONDON REEFS
Pearson Reef
Cuarteron Reef
Pigeon Reef
Royal Captain Shoal
PHILIPPINES
LADD REEF
Half Moon Shoal
Spratly Island
West Reef
East Reef
Alison Reef
Cornwalls South Reef
Commodore Reef
Jubilee Bank
Stag Shoal
Director Shoal
Investigator Shoal
Prince of Wales Bank
Barque Canada Reef
Erica Reef
Owen Shoal
Prince Consort Bank
Alexandra Bank
Bombay Castle
ARDASIER REEFS
Mariveles Reef
Granger Bank
RIFLEMAN BANK
Oriena Shoal
Amboyna Cay
Dallas Reef
Ardasier Reef
Kingston Shoal
Shallow Reef
VANGUARD BANK
Royal Charlotte Reef
Louisa Reef
BRUNEI
MALAYSIA
INDONESIA

consisting of 11 dots, two of which – covering the Gulf of Tonkin – were later removed at the behest of former Chinese Prime Minister Zhou Enlai. Thus came into being the nine-dashed line, viewed by the Chinese government and military officials alike as the historical background for the PRC's claims on the SCS. Interestingly, a study run by the US Department of State, released in December 2014, concluded that China has actually never clarified the jurisdictional intent of either the nine-dashed or the u-shaped line. For China, of course, there was never a reason to assert these claims based on Western jurisdiction.

Paracel Islands

Woody Island – known as Yongxing Island in China – is part of the Amphitrite Island Group in the eastern Paracels and the largest island within this group of islands in the South China Sea. Under PRC control since 1974, it has developed into a military garrison with an artificial harbour and a runway capable of handling military aircraft. J-11BH fighters deployed here in March 2016. (Chinese Defense Forum)

This group of around 30 islands and some 100 reefs, banks and other maritime features has long been a true flashpoint between China and Vietnam. The two countries shared ownership until 1946, when they were occupied by the Nationalist Chinese. Three years later, the PLA conquered the archipelago's main island within the Amphitrite Group, known as Woody Island. In 1954 the South Vietnamese occupied the Pattle Island in the Crescent Group. Tensions rose gradually, before culminating in the Battle of the Paracel Islands, fought between the PLAN and the South Vietnamese Navy in January 1974, after which the PRC established permanent control over the entire Crescent Group, thus completing its objective based on the nine-dashed line. Since 1990, the PRC has launched a number of projects for economic development in the area, including establishment of the city of Sansha on Yongxing Island, construction

of several airports and seaports, and has begun substantial efforts towards land reclamation. The status of Sansha was raised to that of a Prefecture in Hainan Province in 2012, at which time the Central Military Commission (CMC) authorised the Guangzhou Military Command – now the Southern Theater Command – to establish a garrison on the island. The latter is tasked with the defence of the city and maritime operations in the area. In March 2016 the PLA deployed for the first time HQ-9 SAM systems on Yongxing Island (Woody) and probably also YJ-62 coastal defence missiles.

Pratas Islands

Pratas Island is the main island of the Pratas Islands group – known as the Dongsha Islands in China – in the northern part of the South China Sea. Three islets within this atoll are controlled by Taiwan. With no permanent inhabitants, Pratas Island is only visited by fishermen, military personnel and researchers. (Chinese Defense Forum)

Presently a comparatively 'minor' issue within the entire conglomerate of SCS-related disputes, the Pratas Islands (referred to as the Dongsha Islands in the PRC) are a small group of islands and islets and an atoll about 340km (211 miles) southeast of Hong Kong, and 400km (249 miles) southwest of Taiwan. The Pratas are controlled by Taiwan, and since 2007 have been administered as a natural resort known as Dongsha Atoll National Park. A small airport was constructed on the northern end of the island, with a terminal at its eastern end, and this facility is regularly used by the Taiwanese military.

Spratly Islands

Apart from the Paracels, the most hotly contested area in the SCS are the Spratly Islands (known as Nansha Qundao in the PRC; Kepulauan Spratly in Malaysia; Kapuluan ng Kalayaan in the Philippines; or Quan dao Truong Sa in Vietnam). This archipelago consists of around 100 islands, 750 islets, coral reefs, cays, banks and sea mounts, only a few of which are permanently above sea level. They are located in the central SCS, around 350km (217 miles) west of the Philippines, 420km (261 miles) north of Malaysia, 600km (373 miles) east of Vietnam, and 1,000km (621 miles) south of Hainan Island in China.

The area was first claimed by France, in the 1930s, and was later acquired by Japan. Originally uninhabited, no fewer than 45 islands are now occupied and have permanent military installations on them.

A Vietnamese Su-27 overflies Spratly Island, one of the Vietnamese-occupied islands of the Spratly group. (Albert Grandolini Collection)

Fiery Cross Reef – also known as Northwest Investigator Reef or Yongshu Island – lies on the west side of the Spratly Islands within the South China Sea. With about 274 hectares of land reclaimed by early 2016, it is the third largest of the newly reclaimed islands. It features an airport that was completed in January 2016, and is currently the southernmost runway within the area controlled by the PRC. (Chinese Defense Forum)

Most fiercely contested is the northeastern part of the Spratlys, commonly known as 'dangerous ground' due to its countless low islands, reefs, and atolls, and surrounded by rich fishing grounds and – potentially – significant gas and oil reserves. This area is claimed by the PRC, Taiwan and Vietnam, and also by Malaysia and the Philippines. The southeastern part has been claimed by Brunei since 1985. Despite claims and disputes, so far there have only been a few land reclamation efforts beyond construction of breakwaters and piers, primarily around Swallow Reef.

Completed in January 2016, the runway at Fiery Cross Reef was inaugurated by the landing of a China Southern Airlines A319 and a Hainan Airlines 737 on 6 January. State media reported that China is now consolidating its civilian presence on its artificial islands in order to demonstrate its 'indisputable sovereignty' over them. (Top81.cn)

Current possessions in the area can be summarised as follows:

Nation	Number of occupied features	Remarks
Brunei	0	Brunei reportedly operates several oil and gas platforms in the area
China	9 reefs, 6-8 occupied features	While only one of the islands was originally above the surface, at least seven and possibly eight islands have been artificially created
Malaysia	9 islands, 5 reefs, 1 shoal, 3 unoccupied features	Swallow Reef is a 'rock', and other features are unconfirmed high-tide elevations
Philippines	7 islands, 3 reefs, 4 occupied and 29 unoccupied but controlled features	Nine features occupied by the PAF
Taiwan	1 island, 1 reef	The reef is a high-tide elevation
Vietnam	6 islands, 16 reefs, 6 banks and 6 unoccupied features	Up to 17 features with territorial status, all others are low-tide elevations; more than a dozen observation rigs constructed in this area

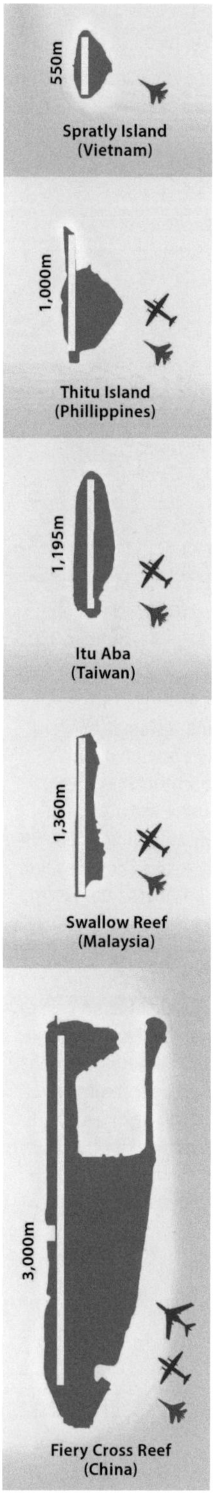

Runway comparison of the operational bases in the South China Sea. (Drawing by Tom Cooper)

Zhongsha Islands (Scarborough Shoal and Macclesfield Bank)

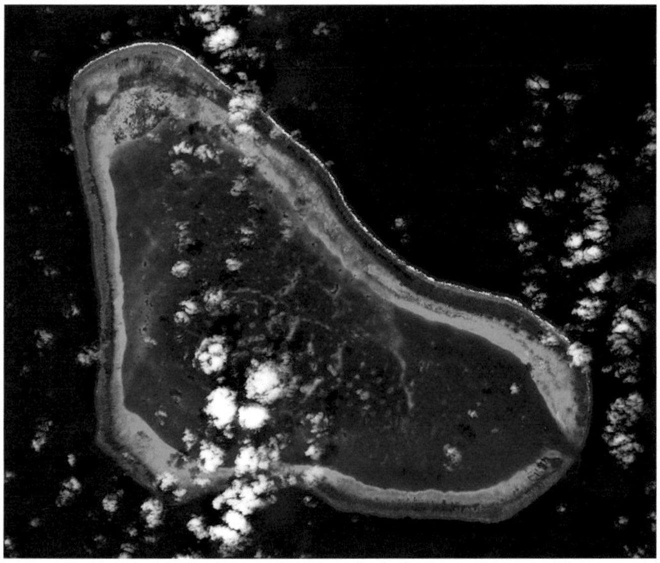

Scarborough Shoal – also known as Huangyan Island – is a disputed shoal located in the eastern part of the South China Sea within the Philippines' 200nm EEZ but under Chinese control since 2012. In early 2016 the US military identified increased Chinese activities that could be a precursor to more land reclamation in the disputed South China Sea. (Chinese Defense Forum)

Literally translated as the 'Central Sands Archipelago', the Zhonghsa Islands actually refer to a collection of entirely submerged banks, islets, sea mounts, and shoals in the SCS. The Scarborough Shoal (known as Huangyan Dao in the PRC and Kulumpol ng Panatag in the Philippines) and the Macclesfield Bank are two major features in the area that form a triangle-shaped atoll. They are around 366km (227 miles) west of Luzon and thus almost in the middle of the SCS, well within the nine-dashed line. The area is uninhabited and only important as a fishing ground.

Since the 'Scarborough Shoal standoff' of April 2012, this area has effectively been under PRC control and access to it has been restricted. According to reports by CCTV, an unmanned meteorological station was constructed here after the standoff.

While land reclamation is usually associated with China, recent images reveal that Vietnam has also been artificially enlarging its islands. Sand Cay – also known as Son Ca Island in Vietnam – lies in the Tizard Bank and is naturally the ninth largest Spratly Island. Occupied by Vietnam since 1974, it lies just 6.2nm east of the Taiwan-held Itu Aba Island. Reclamation amounting to 2.12 hectares was accomplished between 2011 (left) and 2015 (right), especially on the western side of the island. (Sino Defence Forum)

The Macclesfield Bank is one of largest elongated sunken atolls on Earth. It is claimed, at least in parts, by the PRC and Taiwan, but is currently under PRC control, and is administered by the Zhongsha District.

Island reclamation

One of the most fascinating developments in regard to the territorial disputes in the SCS is the large-scale process of 'island reclamation'. Consisting of dredging and building activities on numerous coral reefs, such operations aim to create artificial islands – and thus permanent structures – where previously none existed, with the aim of strengthening territorial claims. Currently, such activities are undertaken only by the PRC and Vietnam, but other countries have announced similar projects.

Although the PRC was not the first to launch such efforts (indeed, it was a relative latecomer in this discipline), it is now by far the largest in terms of the scale of its island reclamation project. Best known under the term 'Great Wall of Sand', Chinese efforts in regard to island reclamation are centred upon the heart of the nine-dotted line, particularly in the Paracels and Spratlys. According to reports from 2015, the PRC had constructed at least 8.1km^2 of new land, but the latest available US intelligence reports describe much more significant construction works, resulting in China reclaiming around 11.75 hectares, Vietnam 32.4 hectares, Malaysia 28.3 hectares, the Philippines 5.7 hectares and Taiwan 3.2 hectares. Much of this construction work is related to the building of airports and seaport terminals, which result in a permanent military presence. The best example of the expansion of Chinese efforts is the creation of the Fiery Cross Reef artificial island, which has eclipsed Taiwan's Taiping Island as the largest in the Spratlys. Currently known military-related major construction projects can be summarised as follows:

Cuarteron Reef – also known as Calderon Reef – is located in the London Reefs, on the western side of the Spratly Islands. Prior to land reclamation – which started in summer 2014 – it housed only a concrete supply platform with communications equipment and radars. In a period of just 17 months between 2014 and 2015, the artificial island was extended to about 23.1 hectares and a lighthouse constructed. (nhjd.net)

Nation	International name	New name	Size (hectares)	Remarks
China	Cuarteron Reef	Huayang Reef	23.10	Access channel, breakwaters, support buildings, helipad, possible radar facility
China	Eldad Reef	Anda Reef	0.00	Construction began in 2015
China	Fiery Cross Reef	Yongshu Reef	274.00	Runway, harbour, support buildings, piers
China	Gaven Reefs	Nanxun Reef and Xinan Reef	13.60	Access channel, anti-aircraft facilities, naval artillery, support buildings, defensive tower
China	Hughes Reef	Dongmen Reef	76.00	Access channel, port, coastal fortifications, four defensive towers, multiple military facilities
China	Johnson South Reef	Chigua Reef	10.90	Access channel, multiple defensive towers, fuel dump, multiple military facilities, possible radar site
China	Mischief Reef	Meiji Reef	558.00	Access channel, fortified sea-walls
China	Subi Reef	Zhubi Reef	395.00	Access channel, piers, runway
Taiwan	Itu aba Island	Taiping Island	46.00	Access channel, breakwaters, new port, runway
Vietnam	Sand Cay Island	Dao Son Ca	2.12	Reinforced sea-wall, defensive positions including gun emplacements
Vietnam	West London	Da Tay	6.50	Access channel, breakwaters, port

A US Navy P-8A Poseidon surveillance aircraft from Patrol Squadron 5 (VP-5) on a mission in the Philippine Sea in September 2014. (USN/Mass Communication Specialist 1st Class Joshua Hammond)

US relations

The official standpoint of the government in Beijing is that most of the construction efforts in the SCS are related to economic purposes, and to 'improve the working and living conditions of people stationed on these islands'. The PRC has never denied that some of this work is also related to defence, and careful monitoring of Chinese construction activity clearly shows indications of a very carefully planned, methodically orchestrated effort which has at least a secondary military purpose. Meanwhile, even the upper echelons of the PLA have confirmed that, while not targeting any country, nor affecting freedom of navigation, the newly created islands serve the purpose of meeting China's defence needs – and are related to Beijing's claims for sovereignty over the disputed area. Based on the latest analysis, China is building up all the artificial islands in the Spratlys for surveillance, tracking and early warning purposes. Furthermore, in the near future the airfields could serve as refuelling and maintenance stations for operations over the SCS and probably the Indian Ocean too.

Because the Chinese construction efforts are viewed with great concern and suspicion by most of the other parties involved, and since most of the countries opposing China in the SCS are US allies, the US is the most serious conflict partner for the PRC in all SCS-related issues. Ironically, while Washington repeatedly cites the UNCLOS as the 'legal basis' for the solution to all such disputes, it has not ratified this convention, and the US does not actually have any of its own claims within the area. However, the US does insist on 'Freedom of Navigation' (FON) rights, and the right to conduct military exercises and 'peaceful surveillance activities' within the EEZs of other countries without their explicit permission. While such operations are in fact permitted by the UNCLOS, they are fiercely opposed by Beijing.

The PRC not only considers peaceful surveillance activities as an aggressive act, but also clearly intends to continue the expansion of its military presence in the SCS. While its present and projected economic and industrial prowess make war against China an unattractive option (except in the case of certain 'red lines' being crossed), and the government in Beijing is clearly uninterested in launching acts of aggression against its neighbours, situations can occur in which certain 'red lines' are crossed. This could be by Chinese or foreign military forces – or it might involve other sorts of situations in which an escalation might be unavoidable.

From the standpoint of Washington, the PRC is not an enemy of the US, but a foreign partner that requires coercive diplomacy. This diplomacy is extremely complicated. While there is no interest in provoking a war, there is a requirement to establish and maintain effective deterrence in order to protect national interests. For such reasons, it remains crucially important to operate surveillance and reconnaissance aircraft in the area – even if these have to be protected – not only in order to challenge Chinese sovereignty claims, but also to demonstrate the freedom of the US Navy to go anywhere it wants in order to demonstrate US military might. Furthermore, Washington is greatly concerned that the PRC might intend to establish an ADIZ over the SCS as it did over the ECS.

Correspondingly, the US military has not only developed plans to reinforce its presence in the area, but also ran several FON exercises in the SCS in 2014 and 2015. The most notable of these saw overflights by P-8 maritime patrol aircraft over the Fiery Cross Reef, and the passage of the guided-missile destroyer USS *Lassen* (DDG 82) close to Subi Reef. However, FON exercises score mere symbolic points at most. Far

from preventing the PRC from building up bases and securing its control over the SCS, they are too little and too late, and are thus unlikely to have any lasting effects.

Combined, this all means that the governments of the PRC and the US face a series of decisions that might decrease or increase tensions. Considering past experiences of decision-making processes in Beijing, it is almost certain that the PRC's decisions will depend on how the US acts first. For example, should Washington decide to bolster its military presence and constantly patrol the SCS with armed aircraft and warships, the PRC might feel prompted to permanently militarise newly created artificial islands. In such a case, the Chinese political idea of a peaceful western Pacific, in which territorial disputes with other claimants are settled in peaceful fashion, might collapse. The early 2016 deployments of HQ-9 SAMs and YJ-62 coastal defence missiles are a clear sign of this tendency.

On the other hand, Beijing could adopt a more tactful approach to foreign relations with other claimants in the SCS, and reduce tensions by making clear and binding statements in regard to its current and projected military presence in the area. This would result in a significant reduction in the US military presence in the area and would increase the chances of a peaceful settlement. Ultimately, the biggest problem for China would be to end up as the common enemy of all its neighbours in the area.

Vietnam

A Vietnamese People's Air Force Su-30MKV2 from the 927th Fighter Regiment lands at Kep air base, armed with a Kh-29 air-to-surface missile. (Albert Grandolini Collection)

Modern relations between the PRC and Vietnam have a long and often troublesome history, dating back to at least 300 BC. The mutual border – which is around 1,281km (796 miles) long and runs through very complex terrain – is based on the Sino-French treaties of 1887 and 1895, which were accepted by the Chinese and Vietnamese governments in 1957–58. At that time, and especially during the US intervention in South Vietnam, during 1960–73, the two countries enjoyed relative good relations and even cooperated on a military level. However, following the PRC's occupation of the Paracel Islands in 1974, and its invasion of Vietnam in 1979, there have been countless disputes between Beijing and Hanoi. In particular, the situation in the SCS experienced several brief escalations, for example during April to June 1994, April to May 1996 and March to April 1997. Some of these almost resulted in armed conflicts. Nevertheless, both governments clearly preferred negotiations to war and relations were normalised in the course of extensive negotiations, resulting in the 'Agreement on the Demarcation of Waters, Exclusive Economic Zones and Continental Shelves in the Gulf of Tonkin', signed in December 2000.

While this treaty resolved all the issues related to the Tonkin Gulf, the maritime dispute in the SCS has remained a matter of intensive but unsuccessful negotiations ever since. The current relationship between the two countries can at best be described as one of 'unstable stability'. Beijing and Hanoi are only in agreement in terms of continuing negotiations over SCS-related issues and are both interested in finding an 'appropriate solution through friendly consultations'. However, a durable agreement over competing sovereignty claims in the SCS currently looks unlikely. This issue is a matter of considerable nationalist pride and emotions, and any corresponding treaty is likely to require a good deal of political faith and courage from leading politicians on both sides.

Lao People's Liberation Army Air Force operates fewer than a dozen Mi-17s, donated by Russia in 1999. (Mariusz Siecinski)

Laos

Laos shares a border of 423km (262 miles) with the PRC. Initial relations between the PRC and Laos were strongly influenced by the latter country being released into independence from French colonial rule in 1953. The original border between the two nations had been ill defined for decades, but in 1991–92 Beijing and Vientiane reached an agreement and signed a demarcation treaty. Mutual relations are relatively good, especially since China provided extensive assistance during the Asian financial crisis of 1997–98. Other positive factors include the signing of a long-term bilateral cooperation agreement in 2000, and the establishment of a comprehensive strategic partnership in 2009. By 2015 the two nations had further intensified their cooperation from economic to military issues. Understanding the geopolitical sway it yields, successive Laotian governments have attempted to maintain a friendly balance between China and Vietnam, regardless of how difficult this might sometimes appear. The PRC's 'Silk Road' strategic initiative is likely to transform Laos into a major transit route to Thailand, turning it into a country of utmost importance for Beijing and perhaps leading to a stronger alliance with China than with Vietnam.

One of Myanmar's MiG-29s returns to Mingaladon air base after a training mission. (Richard Vandervord)

Myanmar

Relations between the current PRC and Myanmar (formerly Burma) can be traced back to ancient times, and are best described as 'peripheral'. For centuries, Burma acted as a buffer zone between China and India, and – except for trade – mutual relations were limited to those between local tribes. The PRC and Myanmar share a common border of 2,185km (1,358 miles), many parts of which were disputed for decades until the Burma-China Boundary Treaty of October 1960, which eliminated all territorial disputes between two nations. Relations during the Cold War were 'cautious but friendly'. Nevertheless, Beijing occasionally complained about alleged discrimination against ethnic Chinese in Myanmar, while Rangoon (meanwhile colloquially known as Yangon) repeatedly expressed concerns over Chinese dominance. The situation began to improve in the 1970s, and especially after a major trade agreement was signed in 1988, legalising cross-border trade. With this, the PRC became one of Myanmar's major economic partners, while treating its southern neighbour in a similar fashion to North Korea during decades of UN-imposed sanctions. Beginning in the early 2010s, Beijing appeared to be getting tired of its continued support, and rifts began to emerge, resulting in the termination of the Myitisone dam project in 2011, several border incidents along the Mekong River, and tensions in Kokang caused by intrusions by China-based insurgents fighting the government in Myanmar. Moreover, the government in Yangon intensified its diplomatic and commercial relations with India and began developing bilateral ties with Japan and other members of the Association of South East Asian Nations (ASEAN).

The Kokang conflict, which began in 2009 with an uprising of Han Chinese against the government of Myanmar, was escalated in March 2015 when combat aircraft of the Myanmar Air Force violated Chinese airspace several times, and one of their bombs hit a sugarcane field in Lincang, killing four Chinese nationals and injuring nine others. The government in Yangon issued a formal apology, while Beijing insisted on a full

investigation and bolstered its troop presence at the border. The PRC clearly prefers to handle this issue with the help of diplomatic and political mechanisms and insists on non-interference in the 'internal issues' of its neighbour. However, considering the increasing flow of refugees over the border, the question remains for how long China can maintain this position.

Capabilities and intentions in South Asia

The PLAAF branch responsible for defence of the mainland coast to the SCS was long the Guangzhou MRAF, which has now been superseded by the Southern Theater Command – the second of two such commands facing Taiwan. Based on the latest reports, the provinces facing Laos and Myanmar have also been transferred from the former Chengdu MR, with the result that the Southern Theater Command is now responsible for air defence from the border of the Fujian/Guangdong Provinces as far as the Himalayas.

While in control of the extensive air defences in the southern provinces of Guangdong, Hainan, Hunan and Hubei, the autonomous region of Guangxi, the Hong Kong Special Administrative Region, and Macau, it was only relatively recently that the Guangzhou MRAF was in possession of the means to exercise effective military control over the SCS too. The most obvious factors in this transformation are the H-6 bombers and Su-30MKK fighter-bombers, which possess an in-flight capability that allows them to reach the Spratlys, for example. Since 2008, the PLAAF has been observed several times over the SCS operating large groups of up to 30 tactical aircraft, supported by tankers and AEW&C platforms. However, the number of regiments equipped with these types remains limited, and this makes the construction of the numerous airfields on some of the aforementioned artificial islands all the more important.

The PLANAF branch responsible for this area is the Southern Theater Command Navy, succeeding the former South China Sea Fleet Naval Air Force. Historically of reduced priority in comparison to the other two PLAN fleets, this branch has recently experienced a major expansion and is currently one of the best-equipped branches

A rarely seen fully-armed J-10A assigned to the 131st Air Regiment, 44th Fighter Division at Luliang. This particular unit was the first front-line unit to operate the J-10 and was reportedly under conversion to the latest J-10C in early 2016. (Top81.cn)

of the PLANAF. It includes not only a regiment each of H-6 bombers and JH-7 fighter-bombers, but also no fewer than three regiments of J-11 interceptors. The PLANAF units in question are known to maintain some of the highest readiness rates within the entire PLA and are regularly seen conducting operations deep within the SCS.

The availability of long-range J-11s and aerial refuelling assets implies that much of the SCS is now de-facto Chinese airspace, or at least that the PLAAF and PLANAF are able to ensure virtually continuous, round-the-clock aerial coverage and combat air patrols over the area during a crisis or a conflict. This is something that no other country with claims in the area is able to match.

In January 2016, two civilian aircraft – an Airbus A319 operated by China Southern Airlines and a Boeing 737 of Hainan Airlines – made the first ever landings at the newly constructed runway on Fiery Cross Reef. While the landing came as no surprise to all parties concerned, it did lead to diplomatic protests from the Philippines and Vietnam, and raised fears that the PRC will be able to take control of the SCS and thus affect the freedom of navigation and overflight. Combined with an increasing number of radio warnings issued by radar stations previously deployed in the area, the landings prompted a number of foreign observers to express concerns that military landings on this and other new airfields constructed in the area are now 'inevitable', and that establishment of an ADIZ is at least 'feasible' – albeit unlikely in the immediate future. Despite official declarations from Beijing that nothing of this kind is currently planned, the PLA is meanwhile expected to begin at least temporary if not permanent deployment in the area of units equipped with types such as the J-11, in turn worsening the tensions by a magnitude.

That said, the PRC has so far been somewhat reluctant to demonstrate its military dominance in the SCS. During the 2012 Scarborough Reef and Senkaku Island tensions with the Philippines and Japan it preferred to deploy its civilian maritime agencies – the so-called 'five dragons' – to directly manage the disputes on a daily basis, while the military maintained a more distant presence away from the immediate vicinity of the contested waters. Indeed, China is continuing the modernisation of its maritime law enforcement agencies and it must be expected that it will ensure they are capable of robust patrols in response to territorial claims in the ECS and the SCS. Some of the ships planned to enter service with such agencies will be capable of embarking helicopters – a capability available to only a few of the current vessels. This implies that Beijing considers the use of military force as an escalatory measure.

The Su-30MKK is one of the most potent operational types in PLAAF service. After their latest updates, these Russian aircraft are also able to use Chinese weapons. Seen here are several Su-30MKKs from the 18th Fighter Division during an exercise. (Top81.cn)

In order to prepare its pilots for missions outside their own areas of responsibility, other PLAAF units are sometimes deployed to the Southern Theater, demonstrated by these JH-7As from the 11th Ground-Attack Division – usually assigned to the Northern Theater Command – during an exercise over the South China Sea.
(Top81.cn)

After years without a dedicated anti-submarine warfare platform, in 2015 the PLANAF finally introduced the first two Y-8Q – also known as Y-8GX-6 – aircraft within a special sub-unit of the 9th Naval Aviation Division.
(F Scan)

Until the Y-20 becomes operational, the Il-76MD will remain the PLAAF's workhorse for heavy transport duties. The PLAAF originally purchased 14 of the type and after a follow-on contract collapsed, China managed to acquire 10-13 additional second-hand examples, all pooled within two regiments of the 13th Transport Division, which also operates at least two Il-78 tankers.
(RAAF)

Southern Theater Command

PLAAF aviation units assigned to the Southern Theater Command
(Successor to the former Guangzhou MRAF)

Code	Unit (division/regiment)	Base	Aircraft type	Remarks
	2nd Fighter Division			HQ Suixi
10x3x (01-49)	4th Air Regiment	Foshan	J-8DF, JJ-7A	
10x3x (51-99)	5th Air Regiment	Guilin	J-10B	Base also known as Li Chia Tsun
11x3x (01-49)	6th Air Regiment	Suixi	Su-27SK/UBK J-11A	
	8th Bomber Division			HQ Leiyang
18x9x (01-49)	22nd Air Regiment	Shaodong	H-6K	Base also known as Shaoyang
10x9x (51-99)	23rd Air Regiment	Leiyang	HU-6	
11x9x (00-50)	24th Air Regiment	Leiyang (unc.)	H-6K	Reportedly moved to Yangtang Li (Xingning)
	9th Fighter Division			HQ Shantou NE
20x0x (01-49)	25th Air Regiment	Shantou Northeast	J-7E	Base also known as Shantou/Waisha
20x0x (51-99)	26th Air Regiment	Huizhou-Huiyang	J-10A/AS	Former 103rd AR/35th Div, coded 4xx6x
21x0x (01-49)	27th Air Regiment	Shantou Northeast	J-7D, JJ-7	May still be at Pulandian
	13th Transport Division			HQ Wuhan-Paozhuwan
20x4x (01-49)	37th Air Regiment	Kaifeng	Y-8C	
20x4x (51-99)	38th Air Regiment	Wuhan-Paozhuwan	Il-76MD/TD, Il-78	
21x4x (01-49)	39th Air Regiment	Dangyang	Il-76MD/TD	
	18th Fighter Division			HQ Changsha
20x9x (01-49)	52nd Air Regiment	Wuhan-Shanpo	J-7B	
20x9x (50-99)	53rd Air Regiment	Changsha	Su-30MKK	
21x9x (01-50)	54th Air Regiment	Wudangshan	J-7B, JJ-7A	Base also known as Laohekou
	20th Special Division			HQ Guiyang-Leizhuang
30x1x (01-49)	58th Air Regiment	Guiyang-Leizhuang	Y-8CB (GX-1), Y-8G (GX-3)	Plus a detachment at Jiaxing
30x1x (51-99)	59th Air Regiment	Luzhou-Lantian	Y-7, Y-8G (GX-3)	Based within the Western Theater Command
31x1x (01-49)	60th Air Regiment – Psychological Warfare Squadron	Guiyang-Leizhuang	Y-8XZ (GX-7), JZ-8F, JJ7A	
	44th Fighter Division			HQ Mengzi
50x5x (01-49)	130th Air Regiment	Mengzi	J-7H	
50x5x (51-99)	131st Air Regiment	Luliang	J-10C	Just under conversion from J-10A/AS to J-10C
51x5x (01-49)	132nd Air Regiment	Luliang	J-7H, JJ-7A	
	Nanning Base			HQ Nanning Wuxu
73x5x (01-49)	124th Brigade	Bose/Tianyang	J-10A/AS	
73x6x (01-49)	125th Brigade	Nanning-Wuxu	J-7H, JJ-7A	
73x7x (01-49)	126th Brigade	Liuzhou/Bailian	J-7H, JJ-7A	
	Hong Kong Garrison			Hong Kong/Shek Kong
6x0x	Independent Helicopter Regiment	Hong Kong/Shek Kong	Z-8KH, Z-9ZH/WH	
	MRAF HQ Flight			Hong Kong/Shek Kong
6x5x	??	Guangzhou/East	Mi-17, Y-7, Z-9	

Forward operating base at Jinjiang

Southern Theater Command

PLANAF units assigned to the Southern Theater Command Navy
(Successor to the former South China Sea Fleet Naval Air Force)

Code	Unit (division/regiment)	Base	Aircraft type	Remarks
	8th Naval Aviation Division			HQ Jialaishi
81x8x	22nd Air Regiment	Jialaishi	J-11BH, J-11BSH	
81x2x 82x3x	23rd Air Regiment	Guiping-Mengxu	H-6G H-6DU	Former 3rd & 2nd BD, not yet renumbered
83x8x	24th Air Regiment	Jialaishi	J-11BH, J-11BSH	Base unconfirmed
??	Unknown UAV Regiment	Jialaishi	BZK-005H	
	9th Naval Aviation Division			HQ Lingshui
81x9x	25th Air Regiment	Lingshui	J-11BH, J-11BSH	
9xx7	26th Air Regiment	Sanya (Yaxia)	Y-7, Z-8J, Z-8S Z-9C	Former 7th Independent Regiment, not yet renumbered
83x9x	27th Air Regiment	Ledong (Foluo NE)	JH-7A	
85x9x	?? Air Regiment or Detachment	Lingshui (unc.)	KJ-500H (GX-10), Y-8FQ (GX-6)	Unknown and new regiment or detachment, first identified in late April 2015, may still be at Laiyang/NSF for final tests

▶ Map of the Southern Theater Command for PLAAF and PLNAF. (Map by James Lawrence)

A PLANAF J-11BH assigned to the 25th Regiment, 9th Naval Aviation Division, during an exercise at Woody Island in March 2016. This is the third naval unit to operate this most capable Chinese 'Flanker' version.
(Top81.cn)

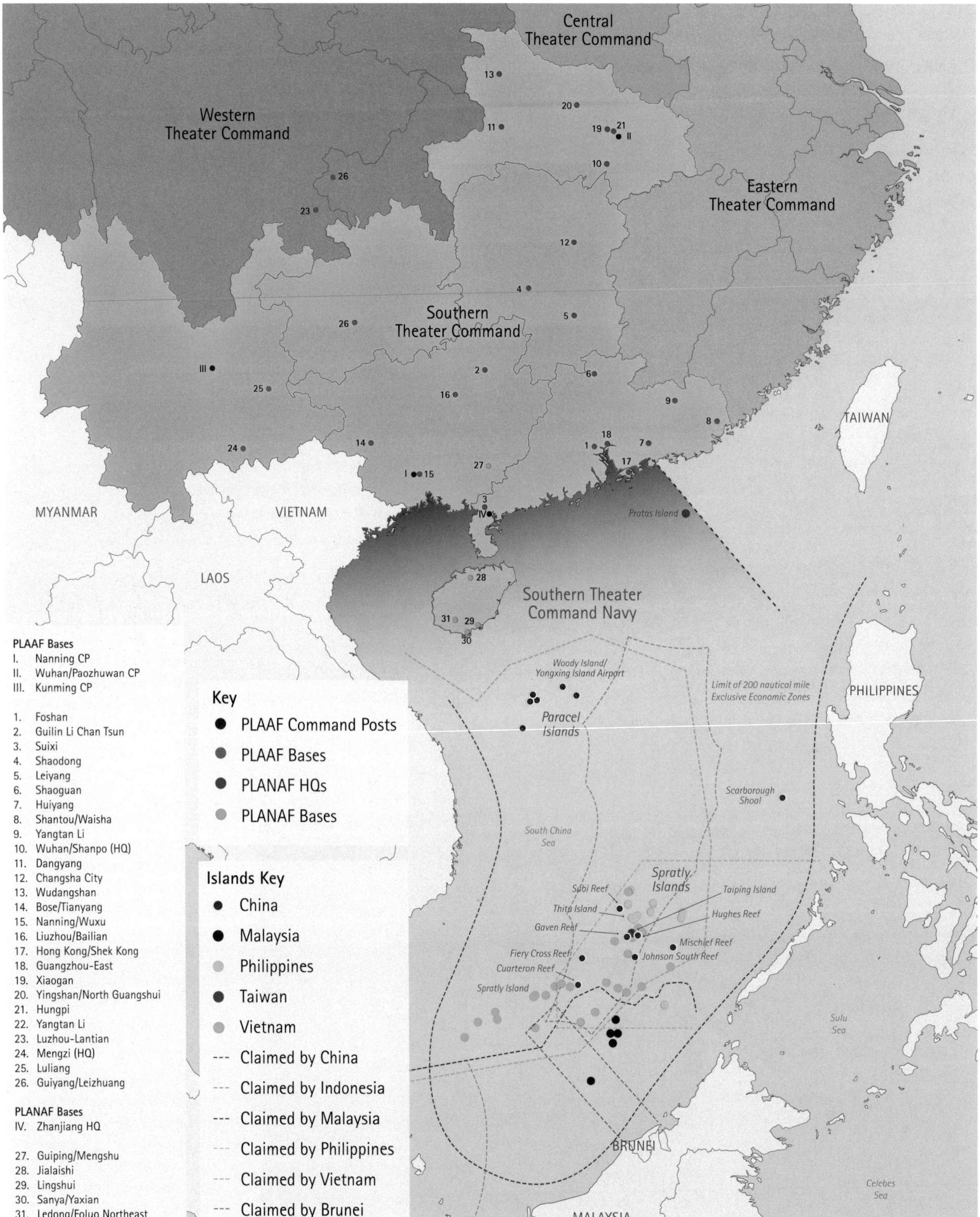
Central
Theater Command
Western
Theater Command
Eastern
Theater Command
Southern
Theater Command
Southern Theater
Command Navy
MYANMAR
VIETNAM
LAOS
TAIWAN
PHILIPPINES
BRUNEI
MALAYSIA
Pratas Island
Woody Island/
Yongxing Island Airport
Paracel
Islands
Limit of 200 nautical mile
Exclusive Economic Zones
Scarborough
Shoal
South China
Sea
Spratly
Islands
Subi Reef
Thitu Island
Gaven Reef
Fiery Cross Reef
Cuarteron Reef
Spratly Island
Taiping Island
Hughes Reef
Mischief Reef
Johnson South Reef
Sulu
Sea
Celebes
Sea
PLAAF Bases
I. Nanning CP
II. Wuhan/Paozhuwan CP
III. Kunming CP
1. Foshan
2. Guilin Li Chan Tsun
3. Suixi
4. Shaodong
5. Leiyang
6. Shaoguan
7. Huiyang
8. Shantou/Waisha
9. Yangtan Li
10. Wuhan/Shanpo (HQ)
11. Dangyang
12. Changsha City
13. Wudangshan
14. Bose/Tianyang
15. Nanning/Wuxu
16. Liuzhou/Bailian
17. Hong Kong/Shek Kong
18. Guangzhou-East
19. Xiaogan
20. Yingshan/North Guangshui
21. Hungpi
22. Yangtan Li
23. Luzhou-Lantian
24. Mengzi (HQ)
25. Luliang
26. Guiyang/Leizhuang
PLANAF Bases
IV. Zhanjiang HQ
27. Guiping/Mengshu
28. Jialaishi
29. Lingshui
30. Sanya/Yaxian
31. Ledong/Foluo Northeast
Key
PLAAF Command Posts
PLAAF Bases
PLANAF HQs
PLANAF Bases
Islands Key
China
Malaysia
Philippines
Taiwan
Vietnam
--- Claimed by China
--- Claimed by Indonesia
--- Claimed by Malaysia
--- Claimed by Philippines
--- Claimed by Vietnam
--- Claimed by Brunei

WESTERN THEATER COMMAND

In common with the Southern Theater Command, the geographical structure of the Western Theater Command has not yet been fully confirmed. According to the first reports from January 2016, it also included Laos and Myanmar, countries normally associated with the typical South and Southeast Asian regions. However, based on most recent reports, the division between the two commands was drawn along the Himalayan states, beginning with India and Bhutan and finally extending to the true central Asian countries including Afghanistan, Pakistan and a second group, comprising the former Soviet Republics. Overall, the Western Theater Command that unites the former Lanzhou and parts of the Chengdu MRs is the largest of the five entities in terms of total area covered.

The second group of countries share very different issues with China in comparison. Based on Western models, one would group these neighbouring states a single unit covering Central and Northern Asia, including all the so-called 'Stans', Russia and Mongolia. However, the Chinese military instead subordinates these countries together with India, Pakistan and the Himalayan states under the Western Theater Command. Consequently, all are covered within this chapter, despite very different historical background and disputes.

In the last 30 years, China's relationship with countries such as Afghanistan, Mongolia, Russia and the various former republics of the Soviet Union – namely Kazakhstan, Kyrgyzstan and Tajikistan – has been one of finding solutions to the various border disputes, some of which date back to the 19th century, maintaining good diplomatic and economic ties, but otherwise not interfering in internal politics. Beijing is interested in maintaining stability and security in Central Asia not only for economic reasons, but also because of the potential instability of the Xinjiang Uyghur Autonomous Region.

Bhutan

The Sino-Bhutan border is 470km (292 miles) long. The geographical and historical isolation of Bhutan from the rest of the world has given the country a unique position in international relations. Bhutan only became a member of the United Nations in 1971, but declined direct diplomatic relations (in the sense of exchanging resident ambassadors) with all major powers for at least another decade. Moreover, because of its deep cultural, familial and religious ties to Tibet, friendly relations with India, and three different border disputes with China, relations with Beijing were frozen from 1959 – when Bhutan closed its northern frontier – until 1984, when the two governments began annual negotiations that have lasted ever since. These talks are extremely complex because of their relations to Sino-Indian and Sino-Nepalese border disputes and related negotiations. Until today, four regions remain matters of dispute between Beijing and Thimphu: around 89km² (34.36 sq miles) in the Doklam area; around 180km² (69.50 sq miles) in the Sinchulumpa and Gieu areas; the border demarcation between Dramana and Zingula; and the border demarcation between Pasamlum and Mela. Both sides maintain that peace and stability are of primary concern in the region, and the PRC began suggesting a concrete exchange of territories in 1988. However, despite 22 rounds of talks, no final decision has yet been reached.

The small Nepal Air Army Wing operates a mix of transport aircraft and helicopters. The most modern equipment is this PZL-Mielec built M28, delivered in 2004.
(Richard Vandervord)

Nepal

Dominated by the Himalayan Mountains, the border between China and Nepal is one of the most natural boundaries on Earth, and stretches over 1,236km (768 miles). Despite several conflicts between the two countries in the 18th and 19th centuries, the border was of little concern to China until officially defined by a diplomatic protocol between Beijing and Kathmandu in September 1950. Despite that agreement, some dispute remained over as many as 20 sectors, until most of these were settled – usually in favour of Nepal – by a border treaty of March 1960.

This was followed by official border demarcation a year later. It was only recently, during the visit of the Nepalese prime minister to Beijing in May 2015, that the issue of a disputed tri-junction of the Sino-Indian-Nepalese border in the Lipu-Lekh Pass area has been mentioned. Although actually related to the issue of demarcation between India and Nepal, the two sides agreed that China should be included in the relevant negotiations.

India

China's relations with India are similar to those with Japan, albeit within a completely different context. The two nations are traditional Asian giants: two of the oldest civilisations, with the world's two largest populations, and now also the two fastest-growing major economies. However, they also share a number of significant and urgent problems, including overpopulation, environmental degradation, mass poverty, widespread corruption and lofty plans to emerge not only as regional but also as global powers. Nationalist pride and two different political systems ensure that they are rivals in terms of diplomatic, economic, and political influence across much of Asia, but especially in regard to unresolved border disputes.

Depending on the definition used, the border between China and India is either 3,380km (2,100 miles) or 4,057km (2,520 miles) long and primarily extends along the southern verge of the Himalayas. Although never officially demarcated, the border was entirely peaceful for thousands of years, but for a host of complex reasons – including competing historical claims, foreign interventions, and the fact that the border is divided into three different sections – it has been subject to fierce dispute since the mid-20th century. Indeed, from the PRC's standpoint, its border with India remains the only major, unresolved territorial dispute, other than the SCS.

The western-most part of the border is in the Shaksgam, in the north of Kashmir. This is not only an area with some of the highest elevations of the world, but it is also one of the most inhospitable. Historically, the Shaksgam area was administered by China, India and Pakistan, until 1963, when Islamabad ceded it to China. Because it claims sovereignty over the entirety of Jammu and Kashmir, India does not recognise the Sino-Pakistani border. The main issue in recent times has been the question of where to draw the demarcation, commonly known as the McCartney-MacDonald Line. This line was the basis for negotiations in 1963, since it followed the natural boundary of the Karakoram Mountains. Although no official boundary had ever been negotiated, China believed that this line represented the accepted boundary. As a consequence, there was little interest in the issue and the boundary remained un-demarcated until India's independence.

The Su-30MKI, illustrated by an example from No. 106 Squadron, forms the backbone of the Indian Air Force. (Angad Singh)

The nearby Aksai Chin area is in essence a vast, desolate and largely uninhabited high-altitude desert, the sole importance of which is that it connects Tibet and Xinjiang. Aksai Chin was occupied by PLA troops during the Sino-Indian War of 1962 and ever since has been administered as part of Hotan County, within the Hotan Prefecture of the Xianjing Autonomous Region. Basing its claims on historical control over the area, New Delhi demands the return of this area as part of the Ladakh District of its Federal State of Jammu and Kashmir. As such, the current official demarcation for the border in this area has not been settled by a bilateral border agreement, and exists only as the informal ceasefire line between both countries after the 1962 war. This line was finally officially accepted as the so-called Line of Actual Control (LAC) in 1993 and again in 1996, under bilateral agreements. Since then there have been repeated accusations from both sides (however, mostly from India against China) in regard to intrusions or even the establishment of camps beyond the actual LAC. In most cases the side accused has denied these.

The geographical centrepiece of the third Sino-Indian border dispute is related to the status of Sikkim. This former Indian protectorate, squeezed between Nepal in the west and Bhutan in the east, was integrated into India in 1975. Sikkim's status has not been disputed by Beijing since 2003. Indeed, the Nathu La is one of only two open border trading posts between the PRC and India. Nevertheless, there is a small part of the border – the so-called 'finger' – that remains the subject of dispute and some military activity.

The most significant border issue between Beijing and New Delhi is the status of Arunachal Pradesh. Geographically positioned in the Himalayas, it is the source of several very important rivers – including the Siang (also known as Tsangpo in Tibet), which becomes the Brahmaputra further downstream – and thus a major potential source of hydropower. Arunachal Pradesh was ceded by the Tibetan government to the British authorities in 1914 following the Simla Accord, which the PRC refuses to accept, since it was not involved in these border negotiations. According to the Anglo-Chinese Convention of 1906, Tibet was not independent from China and as such not permitted to independently sign treaties. The line of dispute here is known as the McMahon Line, which – as agreed by India – defines a border based on the high watershed of the Himalayas. Beijing claimed most of it as 'Southern Tibet' and the PLA invaded the area during the 1962 Sino-Indian War. Although China never relinquished its claims, it voluntarily withdrew its troops from the area. With India insisting on the boundaries as imposed de facto by the UK, and with China refusing to accept these precisely because of the British influence, a solution for this dispute is nowhere in sight.

In general, the unresolved border issues including frequent incursions by Chinese troops into India in combination with the growing economic and military power of both countries will likely ensure they are locked in a security competition in the region.

China maintains an edge over its rival and exceeds India in nearly every respect by such a wide margin that it is sometimes arguable whether it is a true rivalry. The size of China's economy is about four times the size of India's in 2012, and more than eight times the size when adjusted for purchasing-power parity (PPP). China's recent progress in major military developments such as fighters almost dwarfs India's progress in the same field. A comparison of the PRC's military budget, USD119 billion in 2013, reveals that is more than three times greater than India's (USD38 billion). In terms of social issues, including poverty rate (29.8 per cent for India compared to 13.4 per cent for China) and its literacy rate (62 per cent compared to 95 per cent), China has progressed much further.

The problem in this regard is that India's growth in recent years could pose a problem for border negotiations in the future. An interesting analysis by M. Taylor Fravel states that: *'the increasing strength of the* [Chinese] *state in the frontier regions* [Tibet] *suggests that regime insecurity may be less likely to create incentives for compromise'* with India.

A comparison of past negotiations by Srikanth Kondapalli suggests that, invariably, *'China will claim more before settling for less… The so-called territorial concessions that it will probably extend while settling the dispute will not merit being regarded as concessions'*. In several older border agreements – as with the Central Asian states – internal factors often pushed Beijing into making concessions to settle borders issues. However, in the case of the Sino-Indian dispute, *'domestic developments in China could constrain it from diluting its territorial claims to reach settlement… Rising nationalism in China could impede the capacity of future Chinese leaders to compromise on territorial disputes'*, Kondapalli writes.

In general it is fortunate that the chances that either China or India will use force to enforce their territorial claims are slim, especially bearing in mind the countries' generally strong economic ties. Both sides have so far established methods of communication (hotline) to keep each other informed in order to avoid misinterpretations. Both have assured each other that neither side will use its military capability against the other. These measures included an agreement on the guiding principles for settling their long-standing dispute, although progress has only been made at a snail's pace at best. Once again, however, this otherwise stable situation could change, should China deem India's growing relationship with the US to pose a threat. As such, it remains to be seen what role the US will play in this dynamic, and whether it will be similar to US involvement with Japan, Taiwan and the SCS.

Pakistan

The Sino-Pakistani border has a length of 523km (324 miles) and is geographically dominated by a series of high, deeply entrenched valleys through the Kunlun Mountains and the Karakoram Mountains. Historically, the border was first described by the British in 1899, using the so-called McCartney-MacDonald Line, which was clearly laid down by geographical features. However, this line was never acknowledged by the

Chinese. As a result, until the independence of Pakistan and India in 1947, the representation of the boundary varied greatly. Following the first contacts between China and Pakistan concerning the border issue, in late 1959, both states agreed in principle to the demarcation of the traditional boundary. After successful negotiations, the final agreement was signed in early 1963, in which both nations agreed to exchange certain territories.

The new Chinese territory became known as the Trans-Karakoram Tract and this is precisely the issue that is controversial for India. India condemns the treaty as illegal and also claims sovereignty over this land. Importantly, this treaty is specifically described as being preliminary, and that it is to be renegotiated after the territorial dispute with India has been settled. Even if this region is topographically very difficult, this sparsely populated area has a strategic importance due to a number of accessible but vital passes through the area. The region also provides something of a geographical partition between the Muslims of the west and north (Pakistan), the Hindus of the south and southeast (India) and the Buddhists of the east (Tibet).

Pakistan's air defence is maintained by a significant number of F-16s in different versions. Seen here is an F-16AM Block 15 MLU of No. 11 Squadron 'Arrows', on exercise at Konya, Turkey. (Mick Balter)

In recent years the China-Pakistan alliance, initially primarily related to a joint opposition of India, has evolved into a relationship of close strategic allies. This has benefited both nations on diplomatic, economic and military fronts. In other ways it cannot be treated separately and must ultimately always be seen through the prism of complex and interdependent China/Pakistan/India issues. Following the Pressler Amendment of 1990, which led to the suspension of all US military assistance due to Pakistan's development of nuclear weapons, Pakistan developed very close military relations with China.

These were forged not only through the direct purchase of modern Chinese weapons but also in terms of joint development projects such as the K-8 jet trainer, the JF-17 Thunder light multirole fighter, several UAVs and other systems. Besides this military cooperation, both countries are developing the joint 'Pak-China Economic corridor' in order to link Pakistan's deep-water port at Gwadar on the Arabian Sea and Kashghar in Xinjiang in northwest China. This is seen as a key part of China's long-term goal to expand its 'Silk Road Economic Belt' to become a broader economic entity.

However, besides all these positive factors, China has some grave concerns about the unstable inner-political and security situation in Pakistan, and the country has been prone to attacks by Islamic extremists in recent years. For China, this issue is similar to its fight against terrorism and extremism in other neighbouring states, including Afghanistan, Tajikistan and Uzbekistan. However, it is even more problematic, since terrorism originating from Pakistani soil is seen as a threat to its own trouble-stricken Xinjiang Province. Here, the most urgent problem is the East Turkestan Islamic Movement (ETIM), which seeks to proclaim an independent Islamic state. China aims to establish its own military presence in order to effectively counter the Islamic separatists much more effectively than the Pakistani forces have proven able to.

Afghanistan

The Sino-Afghan border has a length of only 76km (47 miles) and is formed by a mountain pass through the so-called Wakhan Corridor that connects Wakhan in Afghanistan with the Xinjiang Uyghur Autonomous Region in China (in fact, the Tashkurgan Tajik

In January 2016 the Embraer A-29 Super Tucano became the latest addition to the new Afghan Air Force. (USAF/TSgt Nathan Lipscomb)

Autonomous County in Xinjiang, China). The border has not been subject to dispute since the Afghanistan–China boundary agreement signed in November 1963.

China has traditionally maintained a low-profile stance in Afghanistan. It has provided assistance to the government in the form of humanitarian aid, financial and diplomatic support, construction of hospitals and roads, and development of water resources. However, Beijing did not participate in the international coalition against the Taliban, nor has it permitted military supplies for the government to transit its territory or airspace. The PRC thus achieved a unique position of not alienating any of the local parties, while making its own investments much less likely to be targeted by the Taliban. Although many countries still hope that in the future China might play a useful role in the reconciliation process between the Afghan government and Islamist extremists, others are concerned that Beijing might fill the void opened by the withdrawal of US forces. Moreover, construction of the Karakoram highway abutting the Siachen glacier to its northeast through the Shaksgam Valley in Aksai Chin – in the Pakistan-occupied part of Kashmir – is of strategic concern for India.

In February 2016 China signalled a potential change in its policy towards Afghanistan, offering the Afghan armed forces increased military aid to counter the Taliban. It seems that the deteriorating security situation combined with the emergence of the co-called Islamic State have encouraged China to take a more active role in Afghanistan. According to Afghan sources, Chinese military aid might include light weapons, aircraft parts and training. According to Barnett Rubin, a former US State Department advisor: *'China now considers the security and stability of Afghanistan as important both for the domestic security of China and for the continuing growth of its economy.'*

The change in policy could lead to military collaboration between the two countries, above all in the field of counterterrorism and training as a means of safeguarding regional security.

Tajikistan

Tajikistan operates just four Mi-24s, which were donated by Russia some 10 years ago.

Tajikistan shares its border with China over a length of 414km (257 miles). A significant stretch of the Sino-Tajik border was not defined and was disputed for many years. Tajikistan is one of the poorest and politically most fragile nations in Central Asia, still recovering from a decade-long civil war. While the border was a source of dispute between the PRC and the former USSR, in the period 1999 to 2002, China reached two agreements with Tajikistan, according to which the latter ceded an area of around 1,300km^2 (502 sq miles) in exchange for China cancelling its claims on another 28,000km^2 (10,811 sq miles). Beijing's concessions were closely related to the surge of violence in Xinjiang Province, and the suppression of Islamic militancy and drug smuggling, but also to the separatist movements active in the Xinjiang Uygur Autonomous Region.

Kyrgyzstan

Kyrgystan's small air force includes just four Mi-24 (seen here) and eight Mi-8 helicopters.

Kyrgyzstan shares its border with China over a length of 858km (533 miles). Contrary to the relatively rapid solution of the Sino-Kazakh border disputes in the 1990s, relations between Kyrgyzstan and the PRC remained strained until the demarcation process was completed in 2009. The primary reason for this was a civil war fought in Kyrgyzstan between 1992 and 1997, and subsequent political instability. The treaty of 2009 resulted in China ceding nearly 70 per cent of the disputed territory in return for Kyrgyz concessions in the regions of Uzengi-Kush and Issyk Kul, which contain not only important glaciers, but also mineral resources including tungsten. Due to ethnic tensions the PRC temporarily closed its side of the border in 2010, but the two governments subsequently reached an agreement for the joint development of a power grid in the border areas.

Despite good cooperation in recent times, particularly in regard to plans for joint anti-terror and anti-narcotics operations, Beijing remains sensitive about the activity of the ETIM, a separatist group of Uygurs accused of attacks in the Xinjiang Uygur Autonomous Region. Predominantly populated by the Turkic ethnic group, Kyrgyzstan has its own concerns related to animosity towards the Uygurs, as well as water supply issues.

Dominated by long mountain chains, Kyrgyzstan is a potential gateway for all sorts of intelligence and military activities across large parts of Afghanistan, China, Pakistan and Russia. This resulted in the US being granted basing rights at Manas International Airport (the former Manas or Ganci air base), from 2001 to 2014, and Russia being granted basing rights at Kant air base in the Ysyk-Ata District beginning in 2003.

Kazakhstan

Kazakhstan operates several upgraded Su-27s from Aktau air base, including this two-seat Su-27UBM2.
(Patrick Roegies)

Kazakhstan shares its border with China over a length 1,783km (1,108 miles). Kazakhstan inherited some of the Soviet border disputes with the PRC, but solved these through a treaty signed in 1994. According to this, a narrow strip of hilly terrain contested since the Sino-Soviet border clashes of 1969 was ceded to Beijing. Two additional treaties of 1997 and 1998 demarcated the rest of the border, in exchange for significant Chinese investment in oil and gas-related infrastructure, and a 15-year economic cooperation programme.

Despite generally good relations between the two countries, ties between the Kazakh people and the Uighurs living in the Xinjiang AR remain a matter of some concern in Beijing. Another issue waiting to be solved is that of water supply. The Irtysh and the Ili Rivers are utilised extensively by both countries, and are a major source for Lake Balkhash in Kazakhstan.

Kazakhstan is a member of NATO's Partnership for Peace project, and has recently made some small-scale acquisitions of Western military equipment and also Wing Loong I UCAVs from China.

Capabilities and intentions in South, Southwest and West Asia

For many years the Chengdu MR, serving as the major PLAAF grouping responsible for the defence of southern and southwestern China, covered the majority of this area (with the exception of the Guanghzou MRAF, which was responsible the border with Vietnam). The Chengdu MR included the remaining parts of the autonomous region of Xizang (or Tibet) and the directly controlled municipality of Chongging. This comprised, de facto, the entire border from northern Vietnam to Nepal. In line with the recent structural reform this already vast area was made even larger, since large portions of the Chengdu MR were merged with the even larger Lanzhou MR. The Lanzhou MR had been responsible for the air defence of the complete Western and Southwestern Sector including the autonomous regions of Ningxia Hui, Qinghai, Xinjiang Uyghur as well as the Ngari Prefecture (usually assigned to the Tibet AR and as such the former Chengdu MR). As a consequence, the Western Theater Command became the largest of the five new theater commands in terms of area. At first sight the military importance of this command might appear limited, since it covers the most sparsely populated parts of China. However, it is precisely here that some of China's most secretive military facilities can be found – including the Lop Nor nuclear research site ('Base 21') and various missile and electronic warfare test facilities as well as the important industrial centre of Xi'an. However, its main importance lies in its proximity to the disputed border with India.

From the standpoint of Beijing, full-scale military conflicts with most of its neighbours in this area are unlikely. One exception is India, and here it is important to state that the PLAAF perceives that the Indian Air Force (IAF) considers itself foremost an offensive arm. Since the 1980s, the IAF has developed into a quick reaction force, expected to deploy rapidly to conflict zones and to be operational along two diverse front lines with very little advance warning.

A J-11A operated by the 98th Air Regiment, 33rd Fighter Division assigned to the Western Theater Command. This unit has also deployed to the Northern and Central Theater Commands, facing Japan, and gained public attention by winning the 'Golden Helmet' fighter contest in late 2014.
(Top81.cn)

One of the few offensively configured PLAAF units in the region is the 110th Brigade, Ürümqi Base based at Ürümqi South (Wulumuqi) and equipped with JH-7A fighter-bombers. (Top81.cn)

For the time being, neither the PLA nor the PLAAF maintains any major units on the border with Afghanistan. The nearest military base is Shule/Baren, housing the seven-battalion-strong 3rd Army Aviation Brigade equipped with different variants of Mi-17 and Mi-171 (seen here), Z-9, and Z-19 helicopters. (Chinese Defense Forum)

The PLAAF has been modernising its transport fleet in recent years. The latest addition is the Y-9, a modern evolution of the Y-8 that was developed in cooperation with the Antonov Design Bureau. This aircraft is one of several Y-9s operational within the 4th Transport Division at Chengdu-Qionglai. (Hunter Chen)

Left: Due to its mountainous terrain, only a few front-line PLAAF units are based in the Western Theater Command. The most important are PLA Army units including those of the 3rd Army Aviation Brigade (Xinjiang MD) operating from Wujiaqu. Six squadrons operate different helicopter types including the Mi-171E (background) and Z-9WA seen here.
(FYJS)

Right: Excellent performance at high altitude makes the Sikorsky S-70C-2 well suited to troop transport and SAR in Tibet and in the Xinjiang region along the disputed Sino-Indian border. Twenty-four Black Hawks were acquired in 1985 and their mission rate has recently improved after being hampered for many years by a shortage of spare parts caused by the US embargo.
(Top81.cn)

Bearing in mind this tense situation, one might expect numerous bases close to India. However, due to its mountainous terrain and difficult weather conditions the Tibet Autonomous Region (TAR) area features barely any permanent, major PLAAF bases. Nevertheless, China has established a dense airport network within the TAR, as well as a series of forward operating bases that could be used in a conflict. Overall, the major bases consist of five airports with a sixth under construction.

Indian sources assume that there are 14 air bases available within the TAR and around 20 airstrips close to Arunachal Pradesh. Even if most airfields are officially used by civil aircraft, all can be used by PLAAF aircraft in case of a conflict, even if the infrastructure of these bases does not currently include adequate facilities for sustained air operations. At the time of writing, neither the PLA nor the PLAAF maintains any major units within the TAR and as such the units are numerically dominated by several battalions of the 2nd Army Aviation Brigade (13th Group Army) at Chengdu/Feng Huang Shan and Chengdu/Taipingsi and the 3rd Army Aviation Brigade (Xinjiang MD) at Shule/Baren, Wujiaqu, Lhasa/Dongguan and Nyingzhi. These are equipped with different variants of Mi-17 and Mi-171, Z-9 and Z-19 helicopters.

Although no front-line PLAAF elements are permanently based here, regular rotational deployments to the TAR are an important part of training doctrine, and these units usually come from the former Chengdu MR. This means that in the case of a war, combat aircraft would first have to be deployed to the area, probably in coordination with a large-scale deployment of PLA ground forces with the help of the PLAAF's transport aircraft, as well as civilian airliners.

▶▶ Map of the Western Theater Command for PLAAF. (Map by James Lawrence)

Western Theater Command

PLAAF aviation units assigned to the Western Theater Command
(Successor to the former Lanzhou MRAF and Chengdu MRAF)

Code	Unit (division/regiment)	Base	Aircraft type	Remarks
	4th Transport Division			QH Qionglai; also known as Qionglai-Sangyuan
10x5x (01-49)	10th Air Regiment	Chengdu-Qionglai	Y-8C, Y-9	
10x5x (50-99)	11th Air Regiment	Chengdu-Qionglai	Y-7	
11x5x (01-49)	12th Air Regiment	Chengdu-Qionglai	Mi-17V-5, Y-7, An-26	
	6th Fighter Division			HQ Yinchuan
10x7x (01-49)	16th Air Regiment	Yinchuan/West	Su-27SK/UBK, J-11	
10x7x (51-99)	17th Air Regiment	Jiuquan Qingshui	J-7B, JJ-7A	
11x7x (01-49)	18th Air Regiment	Lintao	J-7H, JJ-7A	
	33rd Fighter Division			HQ Chongqing-Shashiyi
40x4x (01-49)	97th Air Regiment	Dazu	J-7B, JJ-7A	Reportedly received J-7E
40x4x (51-99)	98th Air Regiment	Chongqing-Shashiyi (Baishiyi)	J-11, Su-27UBK	
(01-49)	99th Air Regiment	Zunyi-Xinzhou (unc.)	J-7BH	May also be at Chongqing-Shashiyi
	Ürümqi Base			HQ Ürümqi
72x0x (01-49)	109th Brigade	Changji	J-8F/G/H JJ-7A	
72x1x (01-49)	110th Brigade	Ürümqi South (Wulumuqi)	JH-7A	
72x2x (01-49)	111th Brigade	Korla-Xinhiang	J-11B/BS	Base also known as Bayingol
72x3x (51-99)	112th Brigade	Malan/Uxxaktal	J-7B, JJ-7A	

Forward operating base at Lhasa Gonggar. Dual-use airports and airstrips available at Ngari Gunsa, Nyingchi Mainling, Qamdo Bamda, Shigatse, Nagqu Dagring.

The latest member of the 3rd Army Aviation Brigade (Xinjiang MD) is the Z-19, which is currently replacing the Z-9WA. The Z-19 is a light scout/attack helicopter based on the well-known Z-9. It features a narrow fuselage, typical tandem cockpit layout and a nose-mounted electro-optical turret. Its main weapons are KD-10 anti-tank missiles (as shown) and PL-90 self-defence missiles. (Top81.cn)

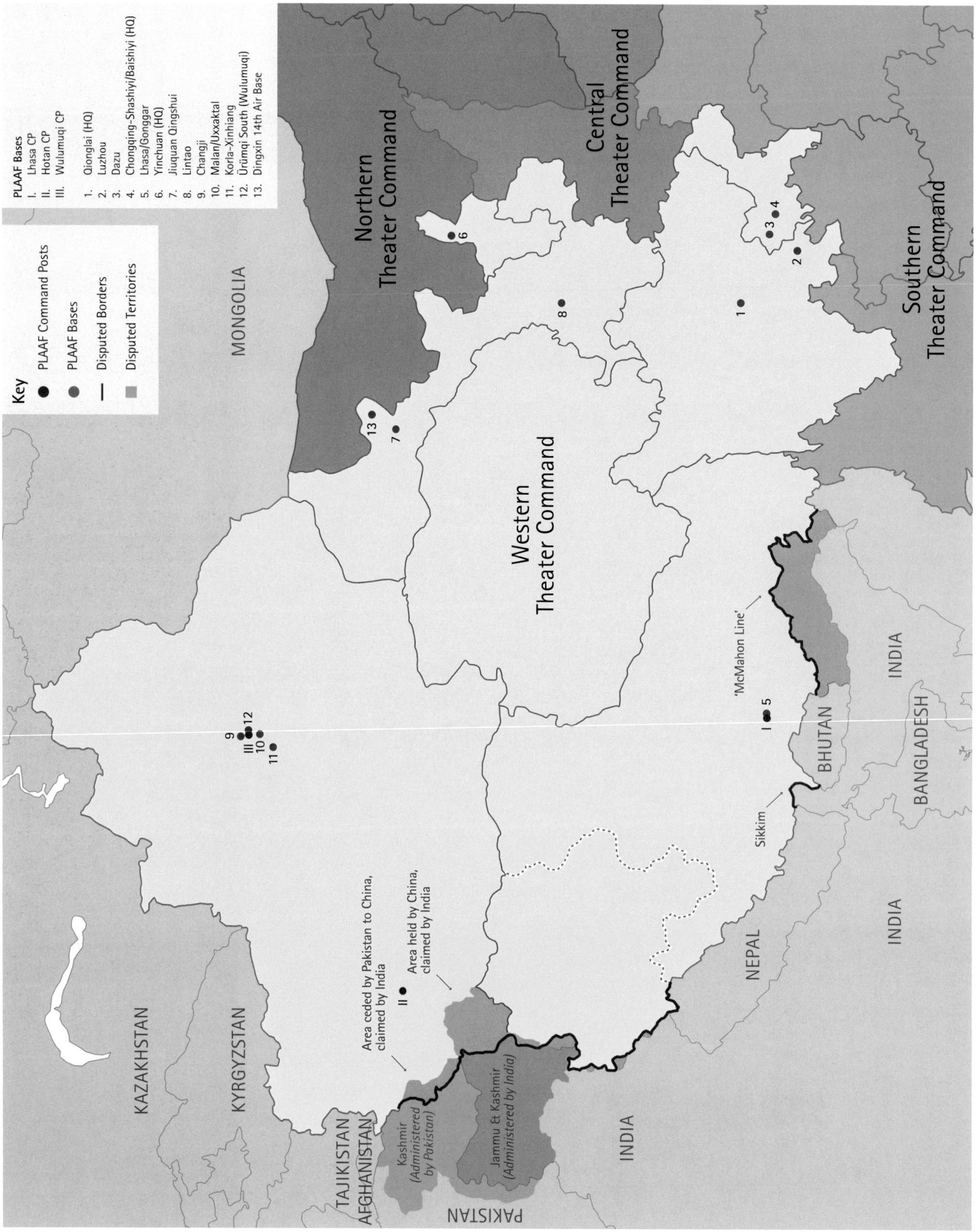
Key
PLAAF Command Posts
PLAAF Bases
Disputed Borders
Disputed Territories
PLAAF Bases
I. Lhasa CP
II. Hotan CP
III. Wulumuqi CP
1. Qionglai (HQ)
2. Luzhou
3. Dazu
4. Chongqing-Shashiyi/Baishiyi (HQ)
5. Lhasa/Gonggar
6. Yinchuan (HQ)
7. Jiuquan Qingshui
8. Lintao
9. Changji
10. Malan/Uxxaktal
11. Korla-Xinhiang
12. Ürümqi South (Wulumuqi)
13. Dingxin 14th Air Base
MONGOLIA
Northern Theater Command
Central Theater Command
Southern Theater Command
Western Theater Command
KAZAKHSTAN
KYRGYZSTAN
TAJIKISTAN
AFGHANISTAN
PAKISTAN
Kashmir (Administered by Pakistan)
Jammu & Kashmir (Administered by India)
Area ceded by Pakistan to China, claimed by India
Area held by China, claimed by India
INDIA
NEPAL
Sikkim
BHUTAN
'McMahon Line'
INDIA
BANGLADESH
INDIA

BIBLIOGRAPHY

Chapter 1

Allen, K. W., 'PLA Air Force, Naval Aviation, and Army Aviation Aviator Recruitment, Education, and Training', *Jamestown Foundation*, June 2015 (http://jamestown.org/uploads/tx_jamquickstore/PLA_Aviator_Recruitment_Education_and_Training_Final_01.pdf)

Allen, K. W.; Blasko, D. J.; and Corbett, J. F., 'The PLA's New Organizational Structure: What is Known, Unknown and Speculation (Part 1)', *China Brief*, Volume 16, Issue 3, 4 February 2016 (http://www.jamestown.org/uploads/media/The_PLA_s_New_Organizational_Structure_Part_1.pdf)

'China and the Principle of Self-Determination of Peoples', *St Antony's International Review*, Volume 6/Number 1 (2010), pp79-102

Austin, G., 'Why Beijing's South China Sea Moves Make Sense Now', *The National Interest*, 16 December 2015

Erickson, A. S. and Heath, T., 'China's Turn Toward Regional Restructuring, Counter-Intervention: A Review of Authoritative Sources', *China Brief* Volume 15, Issue 22, 16 November 2015 (https://twq.elliott.gwu.edu/sites/twq.elliott.gwu.edu/files/downloads/TWQ_Fall2015_Heath-Erickson.pdf)

Fravel, M. T., 'Securing Borders: China's Doctrine and Force Structure for Frontier Defense', *The Journal of Strategic Studies*, Vol. 30, No. 4–5, pp705–737, August–October 2007 (http://www.oxfordhandbooks.com/view/10.1093/oxfordhb/9780199916245.001.0001/oxfordhb-9780199916245-e-027)

Fravel, M. T., 'Regime Insecurity and International Cooperation: Explaining China's Compromises in Territorial Disputes,' *International Security*

Freier, N., 'The Emerging Anti-Access/Area-Denial Challenge', *Center for Strategic and International Studies*, 17 May 2012 (https://csis.org/publication/emerging-anti-accessarea-denial-challenge)

'Hearing: China's Views of Sovereignty and Methods of Access Control', *US Congress*, 27 February 2008

Keck, Z., 'The Political Utility of China's A2/AD Challenge – Anti-Access/Area Denial is often seen purely in military terms. It's much bigger than that', *The Diplomat*, 19 March 2014 (http://thediplomat.com/2014/03/the-political-utility-of-chinas-a2ad-challenge/)

Marshall, T., *Prisoners of Geography: Ten Maps That Explain Everything About the World* (Scribner, 27 October 2015) ISBN 978-1501121463

NOUGAYRÈDE, N., 'The west is trying to understand China, but don't expect trust' *The Guardian*, 26 March 2015 (http://www.theguardian.com/commentisfree/2015/mar/26/west-understand-china-trust-xi-jinping)

O'ROURKE, R., *China Naval Modernisation: Implications for U.S. Navy Capabilities: Background and Issues for Congress* (Congressional Research Service, December 2010)

RAMACHANDRAN, S., 'China Plays Long Game on Border Disputes', *Asia Times*, 27 January 2011 (http://www.atimes.com/atimes/China/MA27Ad02.html)

SULLIVAN, A.; and ERICKSON, A. S., 'The Big Story Behind China's New Military Strategy', *The Diplomat*, 5 June 2015 (http://thediplomat.com/2015/06/the-big-story-behind-chinas-new-military-strategy/)

TAO, Zhang (Editor), 'China's Military Strategy – The State Council Information Office of the People's Republic of China', *Xinhua*, 26 May 2015 (http://english.chinamil.com.cn/news-channels/2015-05/26/content_6507716.htm)

VARRALL, M., 'Chinese worldviews and China's foreign policy', *Lowy Institute for International Policy*, 26 November 2015 (http://www.lowyinstitute.org/publications/chinese-worldviews-chinas-foreign-policy)

WHYTE, L., 'China's Elegant, Flawed, Grand Strategy,' *The Diplomat*, 25 July 2015 (http://thediplomat.com/2015/07/chinas-elegant-flawed-grand-strategy/)

XIE Hong, 'Training and Education of PLA Air Force Pilots in Reform', pp3–6. 'The PLAAF Reforms Its Aviator Education and Training Model', 13 November 2012 (http://news.xinhuanet.com/mrdx/2012-11/13/c_131970220.htm)

Chapter 2

BAKER, R., 'China and North Korea: A Tangled Partnership', *Geopolitical Weekly, Stratfor*, 16 April 2013 (https://www.stratfor.com/weekly/china-and-north-korea-tangled-partnership)

BOEHLER, P., 'China's PLA informed Japan on ADIZ in 2010', *South China Morning Post*, 2 January 2014 (http://www.scmp.com/news/asia/article/1395683/chinas-pla-informed-japan-adiz-2010-report)

CHEN, Qimao, 'Sino-Russian relations after the break-up of the Soviet Union', in CHUFRIN, G., *Russia and Asia: the Emerging Security Agenda*, (SIPRI, Oxford Press, 1999), pp288–291 (http://books.sipri.org/files/books/SIPRI99Chu/SIPRI99Chu.pdf)

FLORCRUZ, M., 'China-North Korea Relations: Beijing Offers Drought Aid Despite Fraying Relations', *Ibtimes*, 18 June 2015 (http://www.ibtimes.com/china-north-korea-relations-beijing-offers-drought-aid-despite-fraying-relations-1973608)

IECHIKA, R., *Nittchu Kankei no Kihon Kozo: Futatsu no Mondaiten/Kokonotsu no Kettei Jiko* [The Fundamental Structure of Sino-Japanese Relations: Two problems, nine decision matters] (Koyo Shobo, 2003)

KAI, Jin, 'A New Normal for China-North Korea Relations - The coldness in China-North Korea relations is more 'normal' than their previous close relationship', *The Diplomat* 19 May 2015 (http://thediplomat.com/2015/05/a-new-normal-for-china-north-korea-relations/)

KWOK, K., 'China and Japan mending frail relationship one step at a time", *South China Morning Post*, 8 January 2015 (http://www.scmp.com/news/china/article/1676613/china-and-japan-mending-frail-relationship-one-step-time)

Lee, Seokwoo, 'Territorial Disputes among Japan, China and Taiwan concerning the Senkaku Islands', *IBRU Boundary & Territory Briefing* Vol. 3, No. 7, pp10-11 ISBN 1-897-6435008 (http://books.google.com/?id=MZGsi1ptLvoC&pg=PA10#v=onepage&q&f=false)

McDermott, R. N., *The Rising Dragon: SCO Peace Mission 2007* (The Jamestown Foundation, October 2007)

Roque, J., 'China wrestles with Russia for control of Central Asia, *China Briefing*, 14 April 2008 (http://www.china-briefing.com/news/2008/04/14/china-wrestles-with-russia-for-control-of-central-asia.html)

Shim, E., 'China fortifying its border with North Korea', *UPI*, 18 June 2015 (http://www.upi.com/Top_News/World-News/2015/06/18/Report-China-fortifying-its-border-with-North-Korea/1731434636934/)

Sneath, D., 'Russia's borders: Mongolia looks to its old Big Brother to counterbalance China', 26. January 2015 (http://theconversation.com/russias-borders-mongolia-looks-to-its-old-big-brother-to-counterbalance-china-36721)

Suganuma, Unryu, 'Sovereign Rights and Territorial Space in Sino-Japanese Relations' (University of Hawaii Press, 2000) pp89–97, ISBN 0-8248-2493-8

Tiezzi, Sh., 'Why Did China Amass Tanks at the North Korean Border? – Was it simply good preparation – or was Beijing trying to send a message to Pyongyang?' *The Diplomat*, 26 August 2015 (http://thediplomat.com/2015/08/why-did-china-amass-tanks-at-the-north-korean-border/)

Tiezzi, Sh., 'China Starts Enacting Sanctions on North Korea', *The Diplomat*, 10 March 2016 (http://thediplomat.com/tag/china-north-korea-relations/)

Volodzko, D., 'No, China Isn't Abandoning North Korea – The idea that Beijing will abandon North Korea remains wishful thinking', *The Diplomat*, 27 March 2015 (http://thediplomat.com/2015/03/no-china-isnt-abandoning-north-korea/)

Xu, Beina and Bajoria, Jayshree, 'The China-North Korea Relationship', *Council on Foreign Relations*, 22 August 2014 (http://www.cfr.org/china/china-north-korea-relationship/p11097)

Chapter 3

Cheng, D., 'Taiwan's Maritime Security: A Critical American Interest', *The Heritage*, 19 March 2014 (http://www.heritage.org/research/reports/2014/03/taiwans-maritime-security-a-critical-american-interest)

Panda, A., 'Chinas 2015 Defence White Paper: Don't Forget Taiwan', *The Diplomat*, 27 May 2015 (http://thediplomat.com/2015/05/chinas-2015-defense-white-paper-dont-forget-taiwan/)

Wu, DD, 'China-Taiwan Relations: Hardly a Crisis – Cross-Strait relations have improved markedly and elections in Taiwan need not reverse that', *The Diplomat*, 31 July 2015 (http://thediplomat.com/2015/07/china-taiwan-relations-hardly-a-crisis/)

Su Chi, 'The history of the 'One China with varying definitions'', *National Policy Foundation*, 4 November 2002 (in Chinese), retrieved 5 July 2008 (http://old.npf.org.tw/PUBLICATION/NS/091/NS-B-091-023.htm)

'Taiwan Matters More to China than South China Sea', *The Maritime Executive*, 17 January 2016

Chapter 4

AMER, R., 'The Sino-Vietnamese Approach to Managing Boundary Disputes', *Maritime Briefing*; Volume 3, Number 5, 2002 ISBN 1-897643-48-9 (http://www.researchgate.net/publication/262726693_The_Sino-Vietnamese_Approach_to_Managing_Boundary_Disputes)

BRUNNSTROM, D., 'U.S. compares China's South China Sea Moves to Russia's in Ukraine', *Reuters*, 26 June 2015

'China Says US Warship's Spratly Islands Passage 'Illegal", *BBC*, 27 October 2015

CHUBB, A., 'The South China Sea: Defining the 'Status Quo' – The 'status quo' in the South China Sea is a slippery concept that does little to advance a rules-based order', *The Diplomat*, 11 June 2015 (http://thediplomat.com/2015/06/the-south-china-sea-defining-the-status-quo/)

DZUREK, D. J., *The Spratly Islands Dispute: Who's on First?* IBRU 1996, pp44–47, ISBN 978-1-897643-23-5

ESMAQUEL II, P., 'Vietnam defends building in South China Sea', *Rappler*, 14 May 2015 (http://www.rappler.com/nation/93189-vietnam-construction-south-china-sea)

FRAVEL, M. T., 'China's Island Strategy: Redefine the Status Quo', *The Diplomat*, 1 November 2012 (http://thediplomat.com/2012/11/chinas-island-strategy-redefine-the-status-quo/)

FREEMAN, Ch., 'Diplomacy on the Rocks: China and Other Claimants in the South China Sea', 12 April 2015 (http://chasfreeman.net/diplomacy-on-the-rocks-china-and-other-claimants-in-the-south-china-sea/)

HAYTON, B., 'Fact, Fiction and the South China Sea', *SeaSearch*, 25 May 2015, (http://www.asiasentinel.com/politics/fact-fiction-south-china-sea/)

HOOD, St J., 'Dragons Entangled: Indochina and the China-Vietnam War' (M. E. Sharpe, Inc., 1992) pp110–118 (https://books.google.de/books?id=3cZ7t3tAR5UC&pg=PA111&lpg=PA111&dq=CHina+Vietnam+border+description&source=bl&ots=PBV-JxI734&sig=kRNIxy_QNeR_v1XKv4Y35MrfHCM&hl=de&sa=X&ved=0ahUKEwiv1Y31ianJAhXRhhoKHbqeDn0Q6AEISTAI#v=onepage&q=CHina%20Vietnam%20border%20description&f=false)

'Island Trackers', *The Asia Maritime Transparency Initiative (AMTI) and The Center for Strategic and International Studies (CSIS)* 2015–16 (http://amti.csis.org/island-tracker/)

'Images show how Vietnam is reclaiming land in disputed South China Sea', *South China Morning Post*, 8 May 2015 (http://www.scmp.com/news/asia/southeast-asia/article/1789136/images-show-now-vietnam-reclaiming-land-disputed-south)

LAMOTHE, D., 'U.S. Navy to China: We'll Sail our Ships near Your Man-Made Islands Whenever We Want', *The Washington Post*, 8 October 2015

LARTER, D., 'Navy will challenge Chinese territorial claims in South China Sea', *NavyTimes*, 8 October 2015 (http://www.navytimes.com/story/military/2015/10/07/china-territory-island-dispute-south-china-sea-navy/73525862/)

'Sino-Vietnam Border Treaties Equal to Both Countries', *People's Daily Online*, 25 January 2002

MEARSHEIMER, J. J., 'China's Unpeaceful Rise, *Current History Magazine 105 (690)*, pp160–162, April 2006 (http://mearsheimer.uchicago.edu/pdfs/A0051.pdf)

RAPP-HOOPER, M., 'Before and After: The South China Sea Transformed', *Asia Maritime Transparency Initiative/Center for Strategic and International Studies*, 18 February 2015 (http://amti.csis.org/before-and-after-the-south-china-sea-transformed/)

Rosen, E., 'What is China Building in the South China Sea?' *Bellingcat*, 22 February 2015 (https://www.bellingcat.com/news/rest-of-world/2015/02/22/what-is-china-building-in-the-south-china-sea/)

Schuette, L., 'Benign or Bellicose? China and the South China Sea: The Ambiguities of the Peaceful Rise Paradigm', *IFAIR*, 15 October 2014

'South China Sea – Mare Nostrum?' *Value of Dissent*, 24 April 2012 (https://valueofdissent.wordpress.com/2012/04/24/south-china-sea-mare-nostrum/)

Taylor, M., 'Regime Insecurity and International Cooperation: Explaining China's Compromises in Territorial Disputes', *Journal of International Security*, Volume 30, Issue 2, Fall 2005 (http://belfercenter.hks.harvard.edu/files/is3002_pp046-083_fravel.pdf)

'Terriclaims: The New Geopolitical Reality in the South China Sea', *Asia Maritime Transparency Initiative/Center for Strategic and International Studies* (http://amti.csis.org/terriclaims-the-new-geopolitical-reality-in-the-south-china-sea/)

Tiezzi, Sh., 'South China Sea Clash Complicates Vietnam-China Meeting', *The Diplomat*, 16 June 2015 (http://thediplomat.com/2015/06/south-china-sea-clash-complicates-vietnam-china-meeting/)

Torode, G.; and Martina, M., 'Tensions Surge as China Lands Plane on Disputed Artificial Island', *The Huffington Post*, 4 January 2016

'UNCLOS III: see Commission on the Limits of the Continental Shelf (CLCS)', *United Nations*, 18 September 2013 (http://www.un.org/Depts/los/clcs_new/clcs_home.htm)

Valencia, M. J., 'US-China Military Agreements Dodge Deep Differences', *The Diplomat*, 10 October 2015 (http://thediplomat.com/2015/10/us-china-military-agreements-dodge-deep-differences/)

Varrall, M., 'How China's Worldviews are Manifested in the South China Sea', *The National Interest*, 16 December 2015

Vu, Khang, 'Vietnam and Diplomatic Balancing', *The Diplomat*, 8 February 2015 (http://thediplomat.com/2015/02/vietnam-and-diplomatic-balancing/)

Chapter 5

Agreement On The Maintenance Of Peace Along The Line Of Actual Control In The India-China Border, 7 September 1993 (http://peacemaker.un.org/sites/peacemaker.un.org/files/CN%20IN_930907_Agreement%20on%20India-China%20Border%20Areas.pdf)

Arpir, C., 'In Bhutan too, Chinese grab land', *Indian Defence Review*, 14 June 2014 (http://www.indiandefencereview.com/news/in-bhutan-too-chinese-grab-land/)

Arthur, G., 'PLAAF versus India', *ANI News*, 7 January 2015 (http://www.aninews.in/newsdetail4/story149068/plaaf-versus-india.html)

Baker, J., 'The Chinese Question in Central Asia', *Caixin online*, 1 October 2014 (http://english.caixin.com/2014-01-10/100627299.html)

Chengappa, B. M., *India-China Relations: Post Conflict Phase to Post-Cold War Period* (A. P. H. Pub. Corp., 2004) ISBN 978-81-7648-538-8

'China/Grenzkonflikt: Trauben des Zorns', *Der Spiegel*, 18 August 1969 (http://www.spiegel.de/spiegel/print/d-45562649.html)

Gomez, Ch., 'China Set to Exert Its Military Influence Abroad', *The New American*, 23 August 2010 (http://www.thenewamerican.com/world-news/asia/item/10278-china-set-to-exert-its-military-influence-abroad)

Hyer, E., *The Pragmatic Dragon: China's Grand Strategy and Boundary Settlements* (UBC Press, 2015), ISBN 978-0-7748-2637-2 (https://books.google.de/books?id=mv6lBQAAQBAJ&pg=PA213&lpg=PA213&dq=Sino-French+Border+Agreement+of+1895&source=bl&ots=2b0YW1R7JM&sig=30odTR6RSdPDGjGCg01vAweYdAY&hl=de&sa=X&ved=0CEMQ6AEwBWoVChMI JXVvduUyAIVC7QaCh3VpQEl#v=onepage&q=Sino-French%20Border%20Agreement%20of%201895&f=false)

Dalal, LTC J. S., 'The Sino-Indian Border Dispute: India's Current Options', University of Madras, 1985; published at Fort Leavenworth, Kansas, 1993 (http://www.dtic.mil/dtic/tr/fulltext/u2/a272886.pdf)

Korybko, A., 'Laos: China's 'Pivot State' in Mainland ASEAN', *Oriental Review*, 4 April 2015 (http://orientalreview.org/2015/04/03/laos-as-chinas-pivot-state-for-mainland-asean-i/)

Kuei-hsiang Hsu, 'A Preliminary Study of the Triangular Relationship between Bhutan, China, and India', (http://www.mtac.gov.tw/mtacbooke/upload/09403/0102/21.pdf)

'Kyrgyzstan and China complete border demarcation', *IBRU News, 17 July 2009 (*https://www.dur.ac.uk/ibru/news/ibru_news/?itemno=8288*)*

Malik, M., 'India-China Relations: Giants Stir, Cooperate and Compete', *Asia-Pacific Center for Security Studies*, October 2004 (http://apcss.org/wp-content/uploads/2010/PDFs/SAS/AsiaBilateralRelations/India-ChinaRelationsMalik.pdf)

Mansingh, S., 'China-Bhutan Relations', *SAGE Journals*, Vol. 30, No. 2, pp175–186, 1994 (http://chr.sagepub.com/content/30/2/175.extract)

'Map: No more border dispute between China and Central Asian ex-USSR countries', *Sun Bin*, 3 November 2005 (http://sun-bin.blogspot.de/2005/11/map-no-more-border-dispute-between.html)

Lewis, M. W., 'The Afghan 'Graveyard of Empires' Myth and the Wakhan Corridor', *Geo-Currents*, 9 November 2011 (http://www.geocurrents.info/place/south-asia/the-afghan-%E2%80%9Cgraveyard-of-empires%E2%80%9D-myth-and-the-wakhan-corridor)

Pearson, N. O.; Rastello, S.; and Tweed, D., 'Nepal Has Powerful Friends in High Places: India and China', *Bloomberg*, 27 April 2015 (http://www.bloomberg.com/news/articles/2015-04-27/nepal-has-powerful-friends-in-high-places-india-and-china)

Ramachandran, S., 'China plays long game on border disputes', *Asia Times*, 27 January 2011 (http://www.atimes.com/atimes/China/MA27Ad02.html)

Rizal, G., 'Bhutan-China Border Mismatch', *Bhutan News Service*, 1 January 2013 (http://www.bhutannewsservice.com/column-opinion/commentry/bhutan-china-border-mismatch/)

Roque, J., 'China Invests in Central Asia Stability Through Tajikistan', *China Briefing*, 22 May 2008 (http://www.china-briefing.com/news/2008/05/22/china-reconnects-with-tajikistan.html)

Rubin, A. P., 'The Sino-Indian Border Disputes', *The International and Comparative Law Quarterly*, Vol. 9, No. 1, pp96-125, January 1960

Sangey, W., 'Would India disrupt Bhutan China Border Negotiation?', *Wangcha Sangey blogspot*, 2 November 2014 (http://wangchasangey.blogspot.de/2014/11/would-india-disrupt-bhutan-china-border.html)

Sodiqov, A., 'Tajikistan Cedes Disputed Land to China, Eurasia', *Daily Monitor* Volume 8, Issue 16, 24 January 2011 (http://www.jamestown.org/single/?tx_ttnews%5Btt_news%5D=37398&no_cache=1#.VdwBpP8Vjcs)

Stanzel, A., 'China moves into Afghanistan', *European Council on Foreign Relations*, 26 November 2014 (http://www.ecfr.eu/article/commentary_china_moves_into_afghanistan634)

Tiezzi, S., 'The China-Pakistan Economic Corridor Gets Even More Ambitious', *The Diplomat*, 13 August 2015 (http://thediplomat.com/2015/08/the-china-pakistan-economic-corridor-gets-even-more-ambitious/)

Verma, Col V. S., 'Sino-Indian Border Dispute at Aksai Chin - A Middle Path For Resolution' *China Indian Border Dispute/World Press*, May 2010 (https://chinaindiaborderdispute.files.wordpress.com/2010/07/virendravermapaperborderdispute.pdf)

Weitz, R., 'Regime change in Kyrgyzstan is largely down to local factors. But it could still have a big impact on geopolitics in Eurasia', *The Diplomat*, 12 April 2010 (http://thediplomat.com/2010/04/china-us-russia-eye-bishkek/)

Zhang, Hongzhou and Li, Mingjiang, 'Sino-Indian Border Disputes', *ISPI Analysis*, No. 181, June 2013 (http://www.ispionline.it/sites/default/files/pubblicazioni/analysis_181_2013.pdf)

Zhao Huasheng, 'What Is Behind China's Growing Attention to Afghanistan?' *The Diplomat*, 8 March 2015 (http://thediplomat.com/tag/china-afghanistan-relations/)

Zhou Xin (Editing by Magnowski, D.), 'Factbox: Relations between Afghanistan and China', *Reuters*, 4 October 2011 (http://www.reuters.com/article/2011/10/04/us-afghanistan-china-fb-idUSTRE79325D20111004)

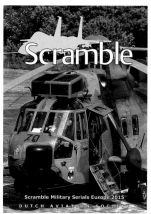

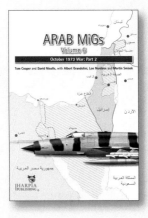